THE MONTREAL POETRY PRIZE ANTHOLOGY

The Montreal Poetry Prize Anthology

2020

EDITED BY

Jordan Abel, Kaveh Akbar, CAConrad, Wendy Cope, Susan Elmslie, Steven Heighton, Yusef Komunyakaa, John Leonard, Eli MacLaren, Marilène Phipps, Sridala Swami, Gillian Sze

THE POETRY IMPRINT AT VÉHICULE PRESS

Signal Editions Editor: Carmine Starnino

Cover design: David Drummond
Set in Minion and Filosofia by Simon Garamond
Printed by Marquis Book Printing Inc.

Dépôt légal, Library and Archives Canada and the
Bibliothèque national du Québec, second trimester 2021.

Montreal International Poetry Prize
www.montrealpoetryprize.com

Published by Véhicule Press, Montréal, Québec, Canada
www.vehiculepress.com

Distribution in Canada by LitDistCo
www.litdistco.ca

Distribution in the U.S. by Independent Publishers Group
www.ipgbook.com

Printed in Canada on FSC certified paper.

CONTENTS

Eli MacLaren

PREFACE

The Montreal Poetry Prize Anthology 2020 is a window into the currents and breezes of contemporary poetry as they are stirring in English around the world today. Opening this book, one finds verdant and various terrain shining, strange buildings, cool airs, and gorgeous scents. There is an apocalyptic ballad, narrating a grisly story of climate change. There is love shimmering in paradox, as in the Song of Solomon, mingling holy sisters and mermaids, haloes and smoke rings, the sacred and the profane. There is a garden with green beans, shiso, and a quiet recognition of racial injustice. There is metaphor clustering three kinds of erasure—a lover's suicide, a solar eclipse, and a grammatical ellipsis—in stanzas reminiscent of terza rima. There is a descent into Herculean myth that asks if poetry is a descent into Herculean myth. There is the astonishing, true story of a woman's surviving a plane crash. These are poems for readers, affording the magnificent views potential within us, ready to be uncurtained.

They are poems for readers, selected for their virtue as crafted works of art that speak for themselves. The Montreal International Poetry Prize was founded as a not-for-profit organization in 2010 by the poet and critic Asa Boxer, with the help of Peter Abramowicz and Len Epp. Every two years it awards a prize of $20,000 for a single poem of forty lines or fewer. Since the beginning, anonymous competition has been the rule. Our database is designed so that the author's name is hidden when a juror reads an entry. The entries are divided evenly among the jurors, who read through their allotment alone and select five for the shortlist. The judge, also working independently, reads the anonymous shortlist and chooses one poem for the prize. "No haggling, no grading, no compromise," Boxer was fond of saying: "this collection is a book of favourites." The pages that follow contain the 2020 shortlist. Every poem here found favour in a distinguished reader's eye.

After running four successful competitions (in 2011, 2013, 2015, and

2017), Boxer sought to give the Montreal Prize a firmer institutional footing and so arranged to transfer the management of it to his alma mater, the Department of English at McGill University. Miranda Hickman, Michael Nicholson, Trevor Ponech, Sandeep Banerjee, and I, together with several graduate research assistants, cooperated to effect this transfer in 2019–20 while mounting the fifth competition. Since *The Montreal Poetry Prize Anthology 2020* marks the first cycle of the Montreal Prize at its new home at McGill, the series title (formerly the *Global Poetry Anthology*) has been changed to reflect this development.

Four thousand six hundred and forty-five entries were received from 107 countries during the 2020 competition. A third of the entries were from the United States, a third from Canada, and the next largest fraction (a twelfth) from Australia. The anthology reflects only a portion of the global participation in the competition but, in addition to the three countries above, includes voices from the Bahamas, India, Indonesia, Ireland, Israel, Jamaica, Kenya, the Philippines, South Korea, Trinidad and Tobago, and the United Kingdom. For one reason or another, the number of entries was over twice that of the 2017 competition. The COVID-19 pandemic was undoubtedly a factor in this increase, whether for its providing unexpected opportunities to write through the weeks and months of confinement, or for its urging existential reflections on love, death, and the state of the world. Regardless of its causes, this surge doubled the workload expected by the jury. Its ten members—Jordan Abel, Kaveh Akbar, CAConrad, Wendy Cope, Susan Elmslie, Steven Heighton, John Leonard, Marilène Phipps, Sridala Swami, and Gillian Sze—all stood up to the challenge, reading approximately 420 entries each and selecting five for inclusion here. Accomplished poets in their own right, they proved their mettle again through the heavy task of sifting through all of these submissions with head and heart, and we thank them sincerely. I shared their labour as a provisional eleventh reader and can attest to the sublimity of what they experienced. Across the world, people turn to poetry to square suffering with hope. The hundreds of entries I read revealed writers young and old framing lines of verse to come to terms with existence. Abuse and abandonment, depression and democracy, genocide and gender, nature and narcotics: these were some of the recurrent themes. Beyond them, every entry was proof of something else—the value of the poem to the average life. Every entry showed someone hammering pain into a rectangular type of courage. To receive these entries was an honour; a trial, to select only a few. To all entrants, we extend our deep thanks, with this message: you are helping to form the community of the Montreal Prize. May this inexpensive book in turn repeat the precept that poetry is for everyone.

It is a precept put better by Yusef Komunyakaa in his poem, "Always a Way," from *The Emperor of Water Clocks* (New York: Farrar Straus Giroux, 2015):

> The flowers always find a way
> into alleys & gullies, up to the shaded
> woods where darkness plays God,
> into the ordinary lives of women
> & men, till *The Potato Eaters*
> doesn't remind them of family
> anymore. Something's about
> to happen in blue, a stolen note
> on the cusp, or chords struck
> across the abyss.

Komunyakaa, the judge of the 2020 competition, author of some sixteen poetry collections and recipient of the Pulitzer Prize, chose "Harlem Valley Psychiatric Centre" by Victoria Korth as the winning poem. To choose one winner from such a shortlist was another trial. We are profoundly grateful for this service, which only a poet of Komunyakaa's standing could provide in a way that all will approve. Korth's poem and his commentary on it may be found in these pages, too.

You will have to search a little for it, though, because, in keeping with past years, we have shuffled it back into the company of the other shortlisted poems, each of which could have won the prize. *The Montreal Poetry Prize Anthology 2020* is intended to celebrate all of the finalists, all of the chords bridging the abyss, all of the flowers finding their way through the allies and gullies. It represents a wealth and diversity of talent in a way that no single poem can. We express thanks to all of the poets for allowing us to publish their work in this book. We hope that you, the reader, will use it to unlock a quadrilateral hole in your wall to see what is happening outside.

ACKNOWLEDGEMENTS

With gratitude we acknowledge all of the labour that made the 2020 competition a success. These efforts have culminated in *The Montreal Poetry Prize Anthology 2020*. The founders of the Montreal Prize—Asa Boxer, Peter Abramowicz, and Len Epp—created a new institution for contemporary poetry in English and we are honoured to continue their work. Miranda Hickman and Michael Nicholson had the vision to bring this institution into the Department of English at McGill University, as the 2018–19 directors of Poetry Matters (a series of poetry events funded by the Social Sciences and Humanities Research Council). The chair of English, Trevor Ponech, approved the initiative at a pivotal moment and collaborated with Ali Martin-Mayer, legal counsel for the university, to complete the transfer agreement, with the blessing of Antonia Maioni, the dean of arts. Prashant Keshavmurthy and Sandeep Banerjee consulted on the goals of the project and reached out to prospective jurors. A team of talented graduate students in English coalesced around the project and advanced it through the work of jury selection, web site construction, records managements, public relations, publicity, and social media activity: Zoe Shaw worked on all of these aspects of the undertaking; Marie Labrosse, Gavin Currie, Jana Perkins, Bahareh Azad, Lehuu Sigler, and Lisa Banks worked on one or another of them. Michael Nicholson devised the new "sponsored entry" policy, which allowed entrants to make a donation to cover the entry fee of a fellow poet anonymously; he also led an extensive and effective publicity campaign. Miranda Hickman coordinated meetings and agendas, identified targets, and liaised with a network of advisers within and outside McGill, including Stephanie Bolster and Karis Shearer. Kevin Lo of LOKI refreshed the visual identity of the Montreal Prize and designed our web site. Martin Evans, architect of the entry database and submissions interface, stood in the breach with brilliant technical solutions to problems that threatened to overwhelm us; no literary prize like this one, funded by the participants' fees rather than endowments, could operate without a reliable online entry and payment system. Pascale Théorêt-Groulx, the audiovisual technician in the Department of English, posted content online and created a striking video to celebrate the prize winner. Brian Lapuz, Sabrina Marandola, and the team at CBC Montreal accorded timely interviews that helped publicize the prize, as did all of the other media contacts listed on our web site. Simon Dardick at Véhicule Press in Montreal generously agreed to publish this anthology, the last record of all of our work in 2020, and David Drummond designed it. To everyone named here, and to anyone inadvertently missed, we express thanks: it has been a privilege to collaborate with you.

Yusef Komunyakaa
2020 Competition Judge

CITATION FOR THE PRIZE-WINNING POEM

The speaker of "Harlem Valley Psychiatric Center" is believable because one senses that the poem was written out of need, out of empathic reckoning. Though the first line reads, "One has to be a little lost to find it," the second line places the reader solidly in a physical space where one is invested and grounded, even if on the edge of a lyrical limbo. This narrator, an intimate witness, immediately becomes a guide, and empathy and inquiry reside in the same register. The poem's tone worked its way under my skin. In fact, it is paramount that the speaker's language is of the real world as she stands in a place where harsh realities have come to pass. The emotional realm may seem almost hidden in plain sight, unembellished.

The title of the poem locates us in "Harlem Valley," which, from the sounds of it, conjures green pastures; yet, the mere existence of the Psychiatric Center corrupts the valley. Though here we are asked to become (as if avoiding the personal pronoun "I") a collaborator through the "speaking eye" simile—the seer, the observer: "Building 85 / still stands. Look it up. Or, better, go yourself." We are invited into the physical architecture, and through accretion the reader enters a psychology of place before we learn: "Its lower story windows broken, boarded..."

The naming of places and things embodies the poem's emotional architecture. And this made thing breathes naturally. Yet, until a certain emotional juncture, there seems to be a looking without seeing. Is it shame? Or, perhaps knowing the fear of being sent "upstairs" to the "glass high-rise..." For a moment, a glimpse of brutal reality, one that is deeply personal, becomes a shared revelation—one that the speaker wishes could be undone. And it is at this moment, the reader becomes not only a spectator, but fully initiated in the psyche of the poem where one almost sees through the speaker's eyes. We know a truth enables this desire to "tear that grim museum / off the map," and with the gesture

—an attempt at erasing the loved one's suffering—one, too, would have to erase oneself. Is the gesture a wish to protect the father or the speaker? This selfless moment makes both the speaker and reader desperately human.

The Battle of the Eclipse

> "There is no suicide in our time / unrelated to history"
> –Denise Levertov

Just imagine: light fading from spears
and desert pinnacles, Lydian & Median warriors
looking to the sky to see their downfall foretold.

Currents of shadow bands fanned
the battlefield as the moon bit through
the sun, a sudden disappearance of day. The war stopped

as three celestial bodies, an ellipsis,
came into perfect alignment. I dream
of all wars that didn't lead to your suicide.

What does it take? What doesn't it take?
There in the sky, your unfinished
life hangs in the cerement clouds.

I keep coming back to it: the way your mind
turned on itself—became war itself—after endless,
elliptical rotations

between here and Iraq. Inevitable
deployments, inevitable danger, inevitable
heat, inedible MREs, incomings,

invasion of phosphorus dreams, insomniac. A fugue
state let slip your own birthright, a boy
looking up at the sky with a pinhole

camera made of cardboard and aluminum foil. Awe
is something so easy to create that we forget.
Any eclipse is worth stopping for…

any suicide is an eclipse.

AMBER ADAMS ❧

Midas

Mother, gold digger of scorched rice, sleep-
sand, overripe banana, coca-cola bottled gasoline,

moonlight tests your fingers positive for
heavy metals, men of iron fists armed

with gold rings, you who found them a delicacy
but believed you could carve bare handed

through the thorn and toughness, taste
a durian's many hearts. You've always loved

to scavenge bones, content with crumbs,
how many times you cracked open sea urchins

mining their golden sex leaving behind empty shells
to the sea, become sand that you would sift

for glitter with a winnowing basket.
Mother, gold digger of treasure hunters, pawn-

shops, fish sauce, betadine on shallow wounds,
beware of fool's gold in cigarette-stained teeth promising

land pregnant with Yamashita's gold and honeyed
cathedrals, necklace undressed to tin in your neck

that you still kiss, rust flavored lips on my forehead.
Mother, gold digger of thrice-used oil, crispy

pata, Joy dishwashing liquid, your body hardening
from their touch, how to convince you there is gold

that sings, not in earth but beneath the eyelids
in a blackout. Our house of light where karaoke songs

run off like heat for we have no need for walls,
where the closest gold I can hold is the shine

of your stretch marks, gold wept in a bedpan
which I pour in the ceramic kiln. Your womb gone

for good. Glory of stitches with nothing to hide,
stiff with God, body hardly touched hard by you

like a rosary bead skipped after decades held
onto. Gold digger of frayed brooms, dried fish,

old chopping boards, 3 o'clock prayers, let me
slow dance you, let me steady your spine

as we leave a trail of gold hairs turning ash in
twilight's blues. Mother of mosquito coil

tongue tips, crunched leaves, rooster's closed beak
on the edge of a nipa-thatched roof, still

clock arms, how much do we have left to lose?

NARO ALONZO ❧

Elegy for a Tiler

When God is still young and of good hearing. When I ask you how one boat could fit two of all living things. When sunflower landscapes of Sicily still bloom the further south you go. When you never see a single sunflower in your aging. When an illuminated road exists on a map, never incised into rock. When mist, like a cloud unmaking Etna at dawn, wraps itself around the overpass so it appears unfinished. When a thousand red shirts envelop the strait of Messina, ceaseless and certain as a wave. When steel migrant ships beach themselves like whales, in Alang, India, bloated hulls of rusted scarlet reef. When the migrant ship, *Gulgluelmo Marconi*, is sold for scrap, liquefied and reborn as an impossible cantilever bridge. When you make yourself very small, each portion of you pooling. When we lap at the folds of your body and the paramedics beat on. When you prepare us for the mystery between wind and water. When it is necessary to know where you are. When I imagine birds with feathers so light, they can only make their nests on the ground. When the Valdaro Lovers and their enduring Neolithic embrace will always be proof that we are binary, show us how we love when we are dying. When monologues transcribed on parchments still reach for the higher plane of meaning-making in their slow violence. When each of the seasons bully their way across your face. When I rewind thirty-five years. When your hair is squid ink black. When your perfect eyes are in vitreous lustre, skin silverpoint, the rest of you, muscle inside glass. When you try to teach me the way of the floor, the way of the trowel, proper proportions of mortar-making, and levelling. When you make me the cutter of the isolation sheet before I can become the cutter of the tile. When I stare into a languorous zoom of mosaic and memory. When you, dark and hulking over the mousetrap, take the spring-loaded bar back, lock the latch, and wait for the sound of the wire to swing down, snapping the mouse's neck. When I dream of tiled floors, the mist of dawn unmaking the volcano and the bridge. When you, made of fire clay, lay on your back on a generous bed of Lungomare sand. When vigil and sleep mean the same thing. When you don't need a priest, who you call the middle-man, to get between you and your God. When your courage is a weapon and a lie. When the surgeon with the skilled fingers of a seamstress, loosens the long thread, picks the garment apart. When Garibaldi and his mille arrive, wrapped in the hill of Calatafimi, red twilight on their backs. When comets, the long-haired stars, leap out of the Sea of Sicily in arcs, guarding the house where you were born and I have never been. When your clean and immaculate feet point skywards. When I see you, half-way across the bridge, complete, unending.

DAVIDE ANGELO ❧

The First Thing I Ever Learned to Draw Was a Bomb

My father didn't know what a bomb was
'till there was shrapnel in his back.

At a pop-up French hospital,
he learned what a bomb could be,
learned what a bomb could take.
A nurse drew a cartoon missile,
three little lines behind it to show it falling from the sky.
She drew a stick figure boy underneath.

He learned then what a bomb could look like.

In the earliest picture I have of my father,
it is a year or so later, and
he is sitting on a grounded missile in Laos,
small boy legs dangling off an unexploded ordnance.
Small boys running and jumping,
playing hide-n-seek around debris.

One time, he said, Komal hid in a hole and found a body part.
One time, Savan jumped on a device
and they learned it only hadn't exploded
yet.

That second time, but not the last,
as they pulled blast from his back,
my father taught all the other boys
how to draw a missile.

Decades later, he taught me too.
We drew the body, and the three lines,
and then a long line across the paper
to show where Heaven forgets Earth.
He showed me how to draw the child on the ground,
arms up in the air,
stick figure hands spread wide, disproportional,
larger than the missile.

Exactly as he remembered.
Hands bigger than bombs.

RA AVIS ❧

Off-World Ghazal

... I could hear
the wild black cockatoos, tossed on the crest
of their high trees, crying the world's unrest.
–Judith Wright, 'Black Cockatoos'

with a nod to Kahlil Gibran & Robert Frost

Are you ready for the round-up, World?
Put your atlas down and feet up, World.

Give me the keys, the GPS. You
thrashed the hell out of the pick-up, World.

What's your pleasure? Horse's Neck, Monkey's
Gland, Cobra's Fang? The night's a pup, World.

Once you were razor-sharp, a Global
knife. Like stainless steel nerve cracks up, World.

Riled black cockatoos cried your unrest
(more than a storm in a teacup, World).

You unsealed records of days and nights
when earth's giant oak was wrought-up, World.

Into fantastic garlands of white
-leaved willow you wove buttercup, World.

You provoked Arctic ice, synthetic
ice, ICE. Your pick never let up, World.

Your coal mind and mechanical eyes
turned the sea of light downside up, World.

Glued to a screen you approved line
-ages', languages', lands' smash-up, World.

Do not move a muscle. I'll freshen
your drink. You look like death warmed up, World.

You built tall walls with stone-boat-loaded
stars thrown from an arc interrup— [World]

You guzzled every *radif* but one.
Your *takhallus* you covered-up, World.

Peter Panesque you gurgled, thought your
-self clever, and never grew up, World.

Thunder, lightning didn't meet again.
In smoke your ambition went up, World.

Umpteen charges valuable as
Mar-a-Lago. Each is trumped-up, World?

A defamation suit? Colourful,
flimsy. In court it won't stand up, World.

No more tricks and abracadabra.
Your fascination is used up, World.

You wish to go the way of all flesh
imperially? A death cup, World.

You won't feel a thing. So long. Farewell.
Arrivederci. Bottoms up, World.

STUART BARNES

The Door

It stands inanimate, unclothed, magisterial
High as it is, a slag of coal dust and light years of musical silence

It lives for every fleeing thing, every word, every stammer, ever knocking sound
The pulpit of pulley and screw pump, and swinging spirals, Archimedes is said
to have named.

The musical sphere of the Pythagorean infant universe stretching its wings,
dream weaving
Breathless frightened shadows, the mares of night that stole the fire from the
Gods

On a wooden crate, in the quiet of the speaker's corner, it barely whispers to the
moon
Minions of metalanguage gird the painter's hand to shade colour shapeless
sapling stars.

Something twists and hollers, glum as a rainy day, that shoe shines the river
eternal
Chasing swallows from the perch of an unfledged twig, a blearing smallness,
tinier than they are

The nested diminutive kingdoms children watch, asking only to be children, for
no reason at all
And the gods, unemployed, by that salvation, and final sin.

On both sides of everything, grimly determined, simply there, as though it were
not
Born of the both of me, where aggregates of thought cradle the circling song

And if I move from my sick bed, as surely the death of death, another morning
flower appears

Though late in the day, it will open and close, the infinitesimals of
angels and parrot fish bloom.

Yet I dream of that door, that is unhinged, to all those who find it glacial in their path
The folly of walking to no other side, stumbling into a barefaced sideling glance

And there, laddering birds, cloistered like creeping vines, sequined silver
Where wingless they march into eternity, the mirror that takes them back.

The blue of the beyond that chimney sweeps the gold
Joual of the jasmine, the rainbow colours of the windswept eye

The azure-winged magpie fluttering, crayoning the metallic taste in our mouth
Knowing the new millennia is the Trojan horse of the old, and older still, the sling of it unborn.

JEFF BIEN ❧

Hold Harmless

Two boys kill half a million honeybees
outside of Sioux City just after Christmas,
the hives smashed, the dead bees clustered
in the snow, and people weep over lost honey
and enterprise, but my heart is occupied already:
a black and white photo of two boys killed
by Soviet partisans at Seitajärvi in July, maybe
six or seven years old, barefoot, their hair
cut short giving them the look of cancer patients,
laid in the dry haygrass, their knees bent up,
but softly, their faces averted, their bodies
not yet vacated in the motherly summerair.

MIRANDE BISSELL ❧

Picking Berries, Belvedere, 1975

Praise to the summers spent whacking paths through blackberry bushes and to our mothers who knew just how much sugar and pectin to swivel in, just how long to let the violet pots bubble and swirl while they tossed back Tanqueray & limes under an evergreen canopy, Mom and bestie Susie from Seattle tucked into the Spruce-dotted deck, late sun slipping away like a child with stolen pantry cake through backdoor screens, light sucking its stomach in, making a skinny ribbon, an echo without a blink. Our mothers sipping their tart, icy drinks while we foraged, gossip and *You'll never believe what happened next* gasped into the last rays casting shade over redwood slats and stripes across their swim-suited chests, rendering them zoo creatures or inmates—cages or heaven—it's hard to say, caught as they were in that epoch's cross hairs, shades of June Cleaver fading under Steinem's bold new strokes, frosty points of their pink toes tapping code against the deck's dark grain, their stifled bursts—laughter or low moans—over a husband's secret deals, affairs, clients gone awry, the leaked lives, domestic baggage unleashed like exotic lap animals between them as cold gin greased vocal strings and volumes rose: signal to us on our return of their liquored, compromised state and therefore freedom to do as we pleased after we'd dumped our brimming pails—bounty left to ruddy immaculate kitchen sinks—sprinting then through shushing sprinklers to rinse dirt and brambles off, cooling ourselves in the high August heat. Our quest completed, one summer, my ersatz cousin Karen came running to where our mothers still reclined, savoring twilight cocktails while dinner's chicken pot pies bronzed on indoor racks, a scarlet band worming its way down Karen's leg as she ran, staining daisy bikini bottoms. *I'm bleeding!* And we thought maybe a rabid bush—berry prick—the tooth of a straggler vine catching her thigh's soft underside in our rush to straddle thorns and snag the inky clumps, little brain-shaped bursts we'd fill our mouths and baskets with, ravenous for the dark marbles, their juicy explosions, like the city's far-off glimmer, its roiling, magical bay. We'd leapt like ponies back to where our mothers cackled on, and now here was Karen doing a little plié, displaying the red rivulets, eyes lowered, overwhelmed. I thought she and I might be sick for a second, excitement and dread for my cousin's first period (how I wished it was me!) while our inmate mothers leaned in to *Ooohh* and *Aaahhh* and grin big at Karen, stroking her rookie cheeks, slurping the dregs of perspiring highballs as furies of forest leaves rustled, circling us in the dusk breeze and we moved inside to help Karen clean up, past the black simmering pots, dipping our pinkies in that stygian, sugary goo—best you ever tasted—sticky and sweet like the news of a daughter's menses we'd jar and seal under layers of thick wax long before the fathers came home.

MICHELLE BITTING

What Gets Noticed

a haibun

At the hospital a man praises an elderly woman, frail and in a gown, for noticing the star lilies out the window. He had not seen them, I heard him say as I hustled past with my son. My mom noticed plenty. My dad's sadness. My sister's struggles. My special son. She noticed dark shadows on my skin when I'd visit at her nursing home. Notice acne and lipstick. She said once, watching my old dog circle, "When Kirin dies, I'm going to go too. I'll go with her." Though she stayed on. Stayed long enough to meet the puppy, sometimes her hand stroking him or patting her blanket thinking it was him. These days, a year without her, my cup too full of grief, I forget to notice things. The trillium blooming in the garden. The softness of things. Forget the green of her eyes in mine. At the hospital my son's specialist discusses weight gain, puberty, iron levels, scoliosis. Does every box in his diagnosis have to be checked? Can't we skip a few side-effects, I think, having dropped him at school before heading to the dog park. The dog notices my mood, scratches at my hand for a cuddle even though I'm driving. He doesn't seem to care. Maybe I'm writing an essay here. I run the puppy round the park, well, he runs me. His excitement makes other dog walkers laugh. One lap takes my entire life or I'm surprised when I come to the fence that it's only my first time around. The sky above is too bright. The hours in the day –

dog wet with dog scent,
my feet muddied
I carry yellow pollen home on my legs.

YVONNE BLOMER ❧

Love Notes from Island Lockdown

To close an island, you must first thread the borders
with bits of sea glass, prayer beads, and rusted metal,
blur the map's blue with your damp open palm.

The coast is half-blind and prone to drifting.
Your island doesn't always come back when you call.
Still, you must forgive its sinking sand
and jagged fault lines. We all have wounds
from which we cannot heal.

But your small house is an island too,
the silver bowl of risen dough on the windowsill,
the sliver of amber in your son's right eye

and sometimes the island surfaces in you,
high and seismic,
like in the middle of this dry month
when the first wave stills
and the mountain poui gasp in yellow adoration.

You want to worship at the peninsula's throat again,
but the weeks and waves still loom
so grey and strange in the distance.

In the sealed container of home now,
Saharan dust clouds drift and settle.
You find airspaces in the secret hollows of trees,
mark time in the nesting cycles of cornbirds
and the fruiting season of mangoes.

DANIELLE BOODOO-FORTUNÉ

Canadian Currents

eroded maple flags
link sea-sick landscapes
fathered by sorry settlers,
sculpting them into capitalist chronicles.

lush prairies hush the Rockies'
wail, cradling knots of gulfweed,
effervescent lakes luring the
blissfully illiterate cartographers.

leisurely, currents swell sunbaked sails,
summer seeping in unearthed soils,
slick ships sink in the ebb,
sanctimonious sprays mothering cornucopian sod.

ancestral earthquakes echo from Awkwasasne
to the Anishinaabe,
white prestige washing up in Canadian textbooks,
residues of residential schools on the shore.

polished wastewaters twist
parched assault stories into sex,
putrid essays on the people's past
buried under debris of patriarchal patents.

welcome signs halt the incoming tide,
iridescent immigration rocks refusing
the flood safety. Canadian turf
reveals its secret saints.

LAURA BOURBONNAIS ❧

Chiroptera: Seven Ages of Juliane Koepcke

& Juliane is reborn through clouds, with a polished coin
under her tongue, no wings. Lightning scrawls history
on the sky; bats cradle her falling, each scream swaddled
in leathery wings. Metal, fire and loved bodies cascade;
her brief infancy is sonar — screeches and rushing air.

& Juliane opens her eyes; the earth reaching for her, arms green
and clothed in leaves, vines twisting and snaking, branches running
through her hair. There is a bone outside her skin, she has been born
from the deepest sleep. Her lips bite together, fish move in the river
confessing water. She learns to walk, lets the mud hold her ankles.

& Juliane moves along the river with a branch in her hand, pushing
from the banks. There are creatures squirming in the red
under her skin. She has doused them in fluid from a metal can.
People are lusting from the shoreline, waiting for her to breathe
so they can write words in newspapers and fill screens with light.

& Juliane escapes to the lawns gripping university buildings; twenty years,
and all the pages she types are bound with fig and fructose.
People cannot hold a conversation with awe; she cannot love people
who drape her body in gowns. She longs for a cloud roiling
with bats, their yawning wings, their faith in science.

& Juliane is a tiny body cradled in the membrane of decades. The bats gnaw
at nocturnes. She stalks caves, listening for the echo of flight, painting
yellow words on wings as they sleep. The bones in her arms are thin
as starlight, longing to be marrowed. Each evening a thousand bats
swirl from the cave-mouth and never worry a hair on her body.

& Juliane flutters eyelashes and people see immortality, a wild man
pretends to wear her skin. He looks at the sky for raining metal

and fills her pockets with chess pieces, promising they represent
something — the way they persist. She sifts through
bat waste, gathering seeds, looking for scratches made by tiny teeth.

& rainforest trees remember the sound of her breaking bones,
under the canopy there are mounds that could be maternal, flesh taken
by leaves. The forest is always hungry and the river is tireless.
She returns the coin to the place under her tongue and lowers
herself into the river-mud, waiting for her mother to fall from the sky.

RICO CRAIG ❧

Early Love as Archaic Landscape

Of my teeth, you said they made me look like a country girl
so I focused on the trinity

of fireflies circling your head. You were a city saint
and had no truck with the backwoods. It's true, I loved

parting branches, the disintegration of fallen trees sidling downhill,
moldy cackle of dried leaves, a collapsed path.

I had journeyed to the foreground
of an archaic landscape to seek my fortune, stone rubble

of what was once home, aflame behind me at the horizon.
I practiced flirtation, gleaned

little learnings, listened as you offered how to pronounce
ebullient, though I wasn't. You wanted me

to move on and I did, cried in the car behind a supermarket
as if alive. Even as a ghost, I hung on, slept

in your cold cottage, ate your co-op cheese, wandered
until I felt blood warming my fingertips, caught

the fox scent of prey, or love, wilding
through a crosshatch of blackberry canes. No need

for the melancholy of abandoned wells, or the bright static
exchange between high clouds, which are in the past and

are immaterial. I returned to the original line, sketched
myself in, blackened the heel of my right hand, the mind

contracting, stretching, to form visible thought:
      I have never been ruined. I am the sum of a thousand ruins.

JANE CRAVEN ❧

César Vallejo Will Never See Winter Again

(Paris in two voices)

FIRST ACT:

Old Vallejo:

This city doesn't know my name. I look at her and know it looks at me. Everyone walks nameless.
The buildings still remember the years of the black death.
Do I exist or am I a failed dream by Eiffel?

Young Vallejo:

I listen to the voices of my ancestors, some sound like my own,
others make me realize that every word I say was thrown away by hundreds, perhaps, thousands.
Everything is born from an internal emptiness that lets me be free like one: man and artist.

SECOND ACT:

Old Vallejo:

I don't know how many times I've died. This body is failing me: my cough is dry, the words are escaping me. Maria Rosa went into the jungle. My
homeland was lost forever.
I try to write my memories. I suffer from exhaustion, I fight, I take the bait to tempt the words.
Everything is futile.

Young Vallejo:

It's useless to write the same things over and over,
I don't know anymore when I give life and when I'm mutilating.

THIRD ACT:

Old Vallejo:

Am I alive? Did they save me at the charity hospital or is this the outcome of faith?
Am I in a nightmare? The news is announcing the Second Great War of this century.
I'm sure I won't see it. My body is shutting down and soon the undertaker will bring me candy.

Young Vallejo:

Yesterday I walked around an unknown city. I got to a grave.
I felt ghosts that forgot their names:
refugees, migrants and gypsies. I walked to a stone that said:
J'ai tant neigé pour que tu dormes
–I've snowed so much so you can sleep–

DAVID CRUZ ❧

Brother in Flight

Look at him, awaiting scrutiny. He's as foreign as you make him.
Already robotic lenses swivel. Perspiration's his constitution, was there
in the damp boy who surrendered in the laundry to a nap—

were you never sheltered where you fell?

I know his eyelashes. Minding his luggage enough to secure it but not
to seem armed. He was a cabbage in a grade school play. Boarding's a perpetual
audition. Now he holds his papers out too early for their talismanic work.

I want you to know what he hasn't done. Hasn't asked for lamb biryani
once last night, his father pounding garlic to a tabla tune. Black cardamoms
smoked over flames. An agent smirked *smell this one?* in a prior queue,

another march through the gullet of his own nation.

Hasn't asked his parents to be here. One goodbye holds all the others
like a Russian doll; opens his mother's floodgates, Ouse, Tana, Jhelum, which river
to even miss? *My boy, my boy*—that prescience of an ending, unaffordable.

He doesn't pray. Relinquishes coins, belt, shoes. Rivulet on his left temple. He
has been separated from his conversation with mercy. He may name
his future children Blake or Jill. The profile of his body scoured of relations,

which is all it takes to kill without killing.

Forget it. Looking at him belongs to me. I did it for love before you ever gave
a fuck. I asked his tormentors *you and whose army*, left a breadcrumb trail through
the briars. If he flies, look at the country forming below his relieved exhale.

SADIQA DE MEIJER ❧

To Find, To Be

awake now: moths shocking the garden
as if bougainvillea or startled white
begonia have taken wing: beds (count them
in the great room empty: kith not yet returned
from last night's excursion up into the bush;
what if? on a hairpin turn: the earth careens
over the crevasse; and now an S.O.S.—
see sky's dashiki or morning iridescence
so much like war confetti over
the triumphal parade? stand. watch. how the hawk-
moth hovers. birds hover. grazing fish hover and
you? does your lovely place treble above mine?
might our dead ride in a car that out-threads
the light's green canyon? might we, its regal tow?

like startled glass; pandemic cans: wind
a caution not to cry: not to rattle
rose-packed chapels with our grief? but hear
the gravel-crunch of tires, the tired
swinging open of the compound gates, thick
lazy slam of all four doors—and voices
like so many bangles, bearing souvenirs: imagine
even the children are safe. cup each one.
touch eager foreheads to your own. consider
what trucks beneath the furrowed wheel: red dust
from the road. crushed begonia. its crowning toll?
the heart's earth-bound watery hack
un-freight red trebles, world: wail your cargo home
if in the garden, nothing, but more moths.

NEHASSAIU DEGANNES ❧

Brexit Haiku

1. Memory

breaks, recedes, then swells:
flotsam of memorials
in Westminster's cowls.

2. Pantry

The gauge siphon slipped:
water for washing up spilled
and spoiled stockpiled spelt.

3. Loose Shy

flailed around our stumps
but scored a century stamped
at the boundary ropes.

4. Autumnal Insomnia

awakes us and Leave
fills the space sleeplessness leaves.
Fall's precipitous.

UMIT SINGH DHUGA ❧

The Square

On the photography of Eugène Atget

Despite their documentary intent, Atget's images
seem to want to be placed in a story.

–Nicholas Mirzoeff

A self-secluded man, he made no claims
for himself, or for the body of work
that imaged dwellings, shops,
whole streetscapes of Old Paris—
many, soon to vanish. And there were
portraits of organ grinders, knife-grinders,

sellers of lampshades, brollies:
as Paris was remade, they'd vanish, too.
Each stands in an unseen spotlight
while, in his singular, patient way
but with Balzacian belief,
Atget photographs them, forever.

And he archived the shanty-towns—
beside a rise of sheds, cabins,
the rag-and-bone men, their solemn-eyed
children looking back at us.
All this with his massive, antiquated
camera, hefted around Paris for decades.

The Surrealists, in their universe of
found objects, discovered him,
prized his pavement displays of
spat boots, cauliflowers, corsets, dolls,
his storefront windows with clouds in flux
above the staring eyes of mannequins.

What he loved most was
early morning light, ashen, sheer,
when the actor, and the painter
he had been, could apprise
then set forth a *mise-en-scène*,
whether spectral and decaying

with playbills lifting from alley walls,
or exquisitely bare, resonant with
the absence of life and lives.
He sets up in a Square, like a silent room:
Eugène Atget, elegist, working on
as if nothing can be truly lost.

DIANE FAHEY ❧

Don't Look

We suspected the tomato thief was a rat but not a mother
of five newborns, now four, fetal and blind to their crushed
sibling inches away on the pavement, where
an evening jogger, thinking they were aborted puppies, picked
each one up and arranged them in the gentle hammock
of her shirt before asking us, "Is this your house?", its tenor
ringing with accusation, as if aware that I had indeed considered, if only briefly,
somehow ridding my young dog of her litter halfway
into her unintended pregnancy,
or of the rat poison tucked into our kitchen cupboard,
and even though I could see those long, limp tails
for what they were, we took the helpless wrinkled and grey things
helplessly from her soft belly into a hard plastic box and then
into our house and placed them on top of the same kitchen cupboard
holding that poison while we decided what to do, out of sight
from their disarming squirms and yawns
reminding me why for years I had a plan in place, like many women do here,
in case of emergency, to head to New York City,
not because I can't, with enough money, find a doctor here
to overlook the law, but because I can't live with my own cruelty
in my field of vision—your ex-wife
knew that too when she took your unwanted strays to the other side
of the island to abandon them, ensuring they would not find their way
back of course, but also so that these ambiguous acts of murder
or mercy could remain within the hard boundary of a carefully-guarded
blind spot, a yawning black mouth of shame and horror
up close, from which your life forever
moves on a deliberate trajectory away, glancing back
in the rearview mirror only to confirm that it grows smaller and smaller until
it's reduced to simply a full stop, a pebble in the road or maybe
something else that your tire silences without ceremony, and you take in
the kind of breath that you know you will hold,

as if your next could either expose or exonerate you, gulping down
the air and with it, the toothless thing that once threatened to swallow you whole—yes
it is always preferable to be in the seat of a car or plane
severing yourself from the unspeakable act, instead of here, in bed,
trying to sleep, while just outside of the gate, where we later returned
the newborns back to their suspected burrow, four heartbeats
grow more and more faint, like war drums retreating
and making their promise to return.

SONIA FARMER ❧

Secateurs

Back in my mother's garden,
the fences were always broken
as the whole of creation clambered in
with tendrils and buried nests
and shanks of love-lies-bleeding.
Star-bright stock, always night-scented,
lit the crazy paving to a fern bank,
where toads with golden eyes
guarded my marijuana crop disaster.
Ivy followed us all the way indoors
with moths that slept in lampshades.
Beetles fell from our homework.
Chrysalides glistened in sock drawers.
Lawns and borders were outlawed
being too needy and English.
Any frost chose its victims sparingly.
Every Spring tasted of honey,
long before the arrival of bees.
Geraniums thrust through rubble
so green was the blade of her knife.
The harder the stem was cut,
the stronger it grew back.
In her hands, life was inevitable
until her fingers grasped only ours
over the bedrail. She coughed
then turned her back once more.
Also, clematis, mint, mallow, foxgloves,
elderberry, phlox and delphiniums.

MARK FIDDES ❧

Birthday Poem

H.F. (father) 9/20/49 – 8/12/2000
A. F. (poet) 8/12/1982 –

I had been thinking of coffins
while lying in my childhood
canopy bed, at 28, watching
Grey Gardens on repeat, the house
folding in and over the mother-daughter
as I folded into the wedge between bed
and wall and thought: baby blue satin
folds of my father's mahogany, or oak
or was it blue, or was the light red upon it?
The areca palm, the lily, or red carnation?
Weak flower of this Ohio. Though I grew
nothing during these years, I thought
of the Pothos crowns from my old place
in Iowa, and the tornado that blew into
the apartment, wrecking leaves, knocking
off plants from hooks: a hole in the room
I could walk right out of—and then what?
Two stories above the spoiled magnolia
I loved without sense, though I knew next
year the blooms would be back three-fold.
My blooms? The night of the tornado, I sat
on the kitchen floor open to stars above
as a grey-blue cloud began to cover each light
like the weathered cedar shake in the Gardens
where you might lie down first, or be laid down
into position from which to beat out of the body
a language like fists, or rocks—this is not
the first time I woke up in a cedar shake

thinking of delicately twisted birthday candles
thinner than a finger, or the blue flame
underneath the light, like the half-moon
cuticles of the little baby I can't have.

APRIL FREELY ❧

Put Flowers Around Us and Pretend We're Dead

The moon arcs—in and out, playing form.
Stars wrap our fate while intruder dreams
signal: come back. They hold our stability with quickened steps.

Stand where grass weaves basket strands, make
the centre heave, the pinched earth speak,
before thoughts erase and we have no names.

Fixed on the busy you miss the owl-winter, the who-cold
crizzling lake. Raindrops inside snowdrops.
When our shoes sprout hello-flowers, cold lips pucker, speak—

What to do but follow this thread? Wind circular words
to chain our necks. A necklace without clasps
means another light's not listening.

To think story is to construct from that other realm
where jade water cools fire's friction. Pockets where pleasure finds memory.
Take this nosegay, touch intuition, before we float off the page.

Now go past sentence. Air-sheets shatter—absorbed
by grasses and creatures scurrying there.
Viral green points down, we watch the swarm.

Swan's neck quickens to question—her wings,
snow-blinding flaps. Nest birds have it—twiggy cup to sink into
after cracking. The rub that brought forth twine and twig weaves the cradle.

Head naked like a freshly hatched bird, moist with dew from the wormfield.
What moves in tawny spurts, jolts. Silence rearranges. It does not mend.
Seed. But know bloom. Unravelling defies gravity. False to think otherwise.

Fools. We have a future to hatch. When roots shoot out—
the sun-calling art of escape: leaf, sepal, petal—the sun
plays hide-and-seek. Silence is a kind of flight.

Scratch light to a rain-flecked level. Twitch strategic to inhabit submission.
Repetition renews. Upland by the railroad tracks—eggs disguised as stones.
Slip past daylight to a time held by skein of old stars—

past evening, past waiting—
Enough! Never enough, until pulled to flight or sleep.
And a dog bounds helplessly wet for a tossed stick he cannot find.

CATHERINE GRAHAM ❧

Category Error

Hummingbirds are fighting
over the flowers in the garden again,
because beauty doesn't make anything
immune to cruelty.

Imagine a world in which each
beautiful creature could be trusted—
and isn't each creature beautiful?

The sleek, streaked coat of the tiger.
The iridescent scales of the snake.
The shockingly blue eyes
of the shooter on the evening news.

LUKE HANKINS ❧

Maybe

If I do all the readings
carefully, diligently annotating
everything that could be important,
researching any words I don't know
for their definition, etymology, useful synonyms
and come to class pencils sharpened,
face washed, hair tamed,
smiling,
papers crisp, notebook open,
textbooks locked and loaded,
raising my hand at least twice
to please the professor,
but no more than four times,
so as not to annoy the other students,
then maybe, just maybe,
people won't realize I don't belong.

CAITLIN HEILIGMANN ❧

The Devil's Bartender

I serve the booze, but know
never to play cards — he always wins,
and every man here owes him money.
He's good to have around —
all those sweaty jokers coming in thirsty,
to cut their deals, clamoring to refill
empty pints and vacant accounts.

Like the rest of them, he can't shut up
about his girl troubles. Goes on
about that first woman, who still won't
return his calls, can't forgive
that long ago madness with the tree.
"Hell hath no fury," I finally say,
laying down another round.
"To forgive, is divine," he says, and then
we both laugh.

Of course, he's got his Daddy issues.
Hated the family business,
hated it so much, he went
into competition. Not the first kid
kicked out of the house, not the first
father to not understand.
But the way he talks
and talks, you can tell
he misses home.

One time, he brought the old man by.
Short, thinner than I imagined,
and although he smiled when I spoke,
deaf as a rock. I poured them whiskey

and listened as the son bragged
about work, the state of the world,
then talked about the good old days
back before the fall. It broke my heart,
to see how much the son
cared, how he rambled on,
as if the old man, nodding, could hear.

AE HINES ❧

Jaani...

...as a favourite aunt
Called you—she took it upon herself to fawn over you the most
Even as you occupied your mother's midriff
As little more than a short longing
For she knew your father wanted girls
To not ride bicycles or wear silver anklets
Like unsubtle whores—
Shortening a *vedic* marker to an endearment in a more poetic tongue,
You, the *gulab jamoon* of her eyes'
Saccharine mist for a feminine child she never had,
Took to food
When lack of masculine predilections
Left you undernourished.

Languishing heavily on a stripped *jamkhaana*
One hot, postprandial afternoon
You lumbered on through laboured breath
Of a drunk uncle who had read
Eighty five years
—eighty three clear and two blurred—
On your palm
Sending me into a panic.

I have caught yours
And gathered my own manly let-downs in whisky glasses
And beer mugs and wine goblets,
Jugs, tumblers, bowls, cupped hands,
Eyes, lies, skies
Until age ceased to be a number.
While I trust my eyes
To peer into yours, my sight may shake
With the affliction

Of the ever-shrinking nineteen years you have over me;
When you push his
Clear prediction—and two more in 'coma splice'—
The idiom of reciprocal tenderness may be worn
Out on the tongues I would have reaped by then.
So, *jaani*, most beloved of aunts,
You must defy uncles
Who are but mere men—
More men.

MAITHREYI KARNOOR ❧

Harlem Valley Psychiatric Center

One needs to be a little lost to find it
on a Dutchess County knoll. Building 85
still stands. Look it up. Or better, go yourself.
Its lower story windows broken, boarded,
but the other thirteen floors appear intact enough
to taunt the empty village outside its gates
with State employment. Our lives, that "campus"
and my journeying, have crossed: first as a child,
and later as a doctor who made some kinds of work done there
my habit, my profession, and today, when heading home
from Danbury in the snow, with no one quite expecting me.
I turned off at Wingdale, followed ditches lined with cow vetch
dropping on the downside of a sudden rise. There:
bakery, laundry, low-slung dorms, brick housing
for unlicensed pharmacists, a minor stadium, and, hidden
in the trees, burial ground with rotting gate and lettered arch—
patients abandoned to the place—every inch dissolving,
stripped of flashing, grizzling with mineral ooze.
And over it all, like speaking eye, the glass high-rise, lobotomy
suite, insulin tubs and narrow beds for the electrically changed.
As my father was, strapped down in '74,
having been there months and shrugging his way
beneath the gaping fence. He told us once he was tired
of trading cigarettes for whiskey in the tunnel
between the dorms, where sex was sold, and coke
and heroin. Said he'd aimed for Armonk, IBM's *mainframe*
where he'd been a salesman, been okay, planned to show up
like Santa in a limo, got as far as Ureles Liquor, collapsed
beside the tracks, was brought back in, sent upstairs.
No wonder he made us stay at the sticky picnic table
in the shade when my mother took us there to see him.
No wonder he was afraid to look the orderlies in the eye,

or so I remember seeing, though it may be
I imagined what I saw, eyes alive with what he didn't tell,
what I felt and what I've tried to know so well
it would unknow itself, unwind to nothing, disappear,
why I am unprepared for this cold fear
and rage—could I tear that grim museum
off the map, would that tear him, tear me in two—
no child should ever be there, or have been, no one.

VICTORIA KORTH ☙

Boy with Thunderfoils

He comes, straight from the stables every day,
over the bridge, joining the others walking
winter's blue-mud lanes, slow trickles pooling
at the gates into a crowd. He crosses through
the yard toward the stage, then goes behind the stage.
A flourish, and a hush, and then he sits. He waits,
motionless, holding the steel tongue of the sky,
muting its cold sharp-edged soliloquy. Peeking,
he sees three thousand faces focused on one thing,
a single action, or a phrase, what's on the stage,
but spilling off, over the whole vast scale of the seen.
He sees the grief of those whose lives are words.
He sees, sitting beside him on the ground, the playwright,
chin in hand, drawing in dirt, mouthing the lines.
Soon he can tell: his moment's close, a charge
brooding the air. And there appears, small, like the slit
of a cracked door, glowing in the distance, in the far
crescendos of grief's song, an opening, a call to shout,
to play, to somehow join the litany, so when the king
at last steps out, screaming and naked, and the boy's
whole body shakes, the sound that comes comes from
within, some faint interior refrain, the pain of his ten years
refracted through these blended gutturals of fire and steel,
the shook-out sound of heaven, of his self, lamenting
his young life, foiling a king, whipping creation into doom.
A noise of keen delirium, of faithless air, making
the older boys, dressed up as daughters, flinch.
He shakes, and grown men wail. He quivers,
and the whole globe swoons. Then he collapses,
sweating, hearing nothing, silence and its sweet threat
stopping up his ears. And then at last, slow baffled sobs.
He breathes. He stands. Exeunt, then home, over the bridge,

past dogs and men sleeping in mud, afraid of nothing
but himself now, of the thing inside of him no king commands,
some mad god buzzing in his bones, a still awed listening,
faint sobbing everywhere, for all time, without end,
poured out of air, landing on everything.

MICHAEL LAVERS ❧

Gramarye

I want speech that makes my skin
more than the book I have made
of its membrane
    silent as lips
    at the mouth
that leans from the air

    and this is how
that work in my flesh began:
the desire that drew me like sap
to its tip, where I hung by my voice
    from the whispering ash
    that grew in the garden
    it made of my death
for runes cut by the tongue to touch
every beginning that is to come
to the egg from which I was born.

I learned to know love by the names that I made
and the names took bodies of their own
that glistered with the dust of their home:
unblinking at the strangeness of what I had done
in piercing their silence, sending my voice
to open as an iris under their sun:
they pluck it from the pulsing earth and come.

I have woken to moonlight leaking from the wound:
    the skin that I speak with
    fresh with the blood of its wish.

GREGORY LEADBETTER ❧

Half-Asleep in Daddy's War

And all our dreams will roll toward the hunt,
some half-asleep dogs mingling behind doors.
My family swallows a habit of barbiturates—
the old spores of war, last years of crumbling
leaves. The wind comes back for us. It stalks.
Whose lungs cracked open in a dream wheezing?

What kind of wind goes off wheezing?
Half-asleep dogs come out of doors to hunt.
Our dream comes back for us. It stalks.
My family keeps a habit of closing doors,
memories of Vietnam come back crumbling
and years have a way of keeping us on barbiturates.

This dream is a body full of barbiturates.
How do sleeping dogs die without wheezing?
We bring back to the dark a habit of crumbling
lungs half-asleep after returning from the hunt.
To believe this family can still walk through doors,
smelling the odor of war, its moldy body. It stalks.

And all of memory will follow us dead. It stalks.
We can't help but beg for our barbiturates
and now the family must lock all their doors
or else nothing is free from the wheezing.
The wind finds a way to carry us back to hunt
as dogs go off again into a dream that's crumbling.

We can't keep us here in a body still crumbling.
There's a love that war stole and it's here. It stalks.
The same way the dogs dig up bones from the hunt
and, no, we can't stop our family tradition of barbiturates.
But don't we lie down sometimes to feel the wheezing?

Sometimes we rise again and open a few doors.
The wind has brought something to our doors—
A memory stacked memory, and oh, it's crumbling.
Will silence come and take away this wheezing?
The family thinks the war is gone. It's back. It stalks.
We think we are safe because we are fed by barbiturates
so let's go now into the mind and bring back the hunt.

Wheezing, it sounds like the opening of doors
and we forget the crumbling that wakes us to hunt.
We hold on to our barbiturates—afraid of what stalks.

BROOKE MCKINNEY

Easter

I got the taste for it
young
under ten
stealing swigs
from bottles
in the larder
I called it the tomb
because every time
I stepped in
and took a gulp
the stone would roll
and I'd walk out
resurrected
anew

It smelt
of the sponge
the soldiers offered up
on good Friday

Two angels
John and Lily
were
in the garden

That time
they thought
chocolate eggs
had made me sick

THOMAS JOSEPH MEALEY ~

Mermaids of the Sacred Heart

They would loll upon the dumpster
behind Wong's Chinese Restaurant
as the light went down on Saturdays,

imagining Sister as the sundown
and the night behind it the young priest
with dusky deep-set eyes.

Smoking and mouthing haloes,
they would sing about illicit love,
what it meant and how it sounded

in seabed songs the radio played.
Sin is never about the act itself
but the timing of the deed. Sex without

marriage was wrong yet tempting,
though marriage without love
followed like a woolly stranger

who begged them to touch him softly
with their youth. Everything
goes wrong as Time permits but they,

in the first verse of their lives, blossoms
of the Rose of Sharon and so belovèd,
blew clouds on which they floated

to wherever life would carry them,
opening their compacts and gazing hard
at lips that kissed the backs of hands.

BRUCE MEYER ❧

Hercules Strangles the Nemean Lion

Parallel geometric planes, each plane a hologram of an ocean's surface, the holographic slices of ocean stacked vertically like the storeys of a building, in infinite series. All motion here is frictionless, inarticulate: you can glide over the surface of a plane until the shadowed horizon recedes or pass through each hologram to the ocean above or the one below. The oceans have a cloudy translucence in which phosphorescent filaments of blue, white, gold, red, orange, and violet glint like the scales of fish. Often the iridescence synchronises across whole tracts of water and you can make out proto-forms in the glimmering churn. But look now yonder: islanded by the fluxing swell, a membrane of water is lighting the rude outlines of a landscape, an encoded mathematical memory of events from eons past: irregular spits of pitchy rock forked in the gritty, weedy soil of an olive-hued scrubland beneath a bleached, cancelling sky.

Extruding ribcages of mauled oxen sticky with congealed blood and swarming with blue-green flies lie between tufts of wild grass, and a shepherd's dog is barking dementedly, and bubbles of blood inflate and deflate on the lips of a shepherd boy who is still alive, his eyeballs, brow, and the bridge of his nose torn from his face, and something is loping in the periphery, its mane and head dark umber and slick with blood, and it has been chased twice on horseback and pelted with arrows and stones back to its cave a league distant from the nearest settlement, but it smells the sweat of the livestock on the breeze.

His greaves jag into the flesh of his ankles as he pounds uphill, the loose chalky topsoil giving way underfoot and scattering backwards in dusty cones. In his right hand is a truculent wooden club honey-combed with dull nails, the weighted end pointing downwards like a third leg or a pendulum, which he periodically drives into the earth whilst climbing to keep his footing. Nearing the crescent lips of the cave mouth he relaxes his pace, uncords his vast shield from his back, and rights his club. The entranceway is hooded like a monk's cowl, and he sidles through it while his eyes adjust to the grainy darkness inside. Amid the black organs of the chamber he sees two golden zeroes hanging in mid-air, and with its long, shadowed, rutted face it is as though the luminescent eyes of some minor rustic deity are peering from behind a carved wooden mask. He rushes it with his shield, hoping to lame its front legs with his club before it can react, but it is lying atop a flat-topped, chest-high rock, and as he raises his club it throws itself at his head and lands on his shield and clings to his shield's top edge with one paw and with the other paw swipes at the arm holding the club, and ribbons of flesh open on his forearm and he drops the club, and its claws lacerate his bowed neck and shoulders as he carries it clinging to his shield like some monstrous baby and slams its back against the cave wall. With its limbs pinned and splayed under the bronze oval, he starts thumping its head with the bottom of his fist like a shipwright nailing planks into a ship's hull. After twenty blows it writhes free and with its bloodied head makes for the white pool of the cave mouth. He throws aside his shield and jumps on its back. He reaches around the soft underside of its huge neck with his right arm and with his left hand palming the back of his right hand grapples it into a chokehold, and it struggles demonically, but null its face and claws it is nothing but blind, striated ropes of muscle pulling on rods of bone, and his face is pressed into its matted mane and he breathes the hot musk of its body as its life ebbs away.

MAX MITCHELL ❧

At the Met to Get Wrecked

I wander the monuments in the Empire State and do not think
of victims, per se; larceny, per se; scale, per se. I'm hurting—
I just want to not be part of something, this thing; I want a good,
beautiful song. In the Met are the good things, endowments
that purchase the painted flowers, the nude female bodies,
but these form the detritus of time—privilege fanning itself,
saying: *I take, and take, and take, me o my o me o my*—therefore
perfect for the Empire State and its crowds. No. I gravitate
to one sad and broken scene reproduced over and over—the family.
How to take in The Family as *objet*? How does one scan Manets?
Degases? Van Goghs? One does, if one is pulled to canvases
with families. Forgotten – bare flesh, epic combat scenes, landscapes.
Then I see: the fatherless, the motherless, scene with children aged
like mine—Picasso's "La Coiffure." Do you know why you stood
at the altar, really? Isn't there mystery at the core of metaphor?
I was summoned here to not-understand, to wonder at how the children
are comfortable with each other. A domesticity of foreground, no home
or other life; the boy's face at an odd slant, as if he, too, is tilted at the angle
of the world, and the girls so carefully grooming beauty—the eldest
arranging the middle child's hair, the middle child holding onto a blank
mirror with both hands. I could tell you we're the lack of background,
we're the mirror that won't reflect; more ekphrasis can be done. But
my problem's here: the entire regiment of my body wants to protect
these children, to let them be with one another unharmed; but I would
want to be background, and that would ruin the picture. *I love you,*
my family! It is love that I feel, with every rough gesture and word!
May I save you? I may not, there is no background for that. Que sera,
Doris Day sings to my son's temporal lobes, Que sera. There's only
the boy in his own self, disinterested in his sisters and the background,
and yet parallel to them. *Is he sad?* is my constant question and worry.
What does he know? Does he know more than me? He is in the picture,
next to beauty—closer than I will ever get, protected.

SHANE NEILSON ❧

First Time at The Airport

When I carry my passport I bring along a certain smell with it
the smell of galangal chicken slow-cooked over a dawn looming
with solemn adhan by the hands of a sleepless, clueless mother
who doesn't know her daughter will be fed by a cabin crew, by

someone's mother who politely hands out italicised menu with a
sleepless smile paralleling her own, my mom—she doesn't know how
capitalism works, only ways to survive in it, only knows her
seven-to-five, bogus-brand stilettos and excel spreadsheets

only knows love   and love   for no reason, only the
tedious things she mistook for devotion, the comfort she gets
from ripping monthly bills she has paid. I get more comfort
from pouring the scatter from the bin and piece them together

like a puzzle. Who wants to picture a faraway Eiffel tower when
you can piece together your utilities consumption? No—no faraway
land is farther than a life lit with fire. As it smears the hands
of its beholders with sharp galangal smell, my passport's parting

ways ahead of me like God parting the Red Sea for Moses
like a general in a journey of conquest, it clears the path for me to
stride   and stride   forward in a line of people
crossing boundaries I feel like an island contracting, closing chasm

with my elbows I keep gently expanding, I remember those bedtime
whispers when my mother used to say *boundaries are myths*, I mull
over it while we're crowding here still bodies dovetailing, waiting
for a band of strangers pointing at the lines we shall never cross—

DIANTY NINGRUM ❧

Bookend to a Flood

Sky empty of clouds and we chew stubble for weeks
until he tells me we are leaving, but there is nowhere,
the Earth is evaporating into dust and desperation.

The drought reveals the land's knapped skull,
skinned to a grin of granite teeth, the end
of the Earth begins with dust and dubious gifts:

hulls on their blocks, beached beyond any ocean,
piers over dunes far from their tepid shores, the
acid retreat of water, the last days of petrification,

and things better hidden, rummaged into corners,
or drowned for forgetting: dented barrels, wrecks and
disasters, surreptitious concealments, sunken treasure.

The day before we abandoned hope, tossing it like a
wriggling bag of kittens, the scouring dried the middle
of the dam and we could see a bleached and bloated suitcase.

Nothing given over to the nip of eels and poke of turtles
blankly nudging, can do a man good, can re-pour the water
or populate the ossification of our town, dead of thirst,

but my husband dragged it to the cracked margins of the dam
grunting about salvage and stood staring at it with
the raw eyes of a fortune teller whose card will not turn.

I thought of Pandora cupping shadows and a curse, I
thought of the emptiness to be found in a Magician's hat, I
thought of the bundles buried underneath a silent threshold.

He broke the old locks and swore at the contents, stumbling
from the bones of a little girl sleeping, here in the water of
the district's last dam. Now there's truly nothing to hold us.

I wonder how long she huddled in there drowning, while the
great drought baked us, and how long in turn will the wind
push us to wander. Until rain falls again to cover all our secrets.

DAMEN O'BRIEN ❧

Still & Quiet Things

Somewhere in the Midlands a newly bereaved husband sits watching television with his three small children. A couple plants Jerusalem artichokes on their allotment in Zone 6. Up and down a street in Bromley, a window cleaner overhears family arguments. In Wiltshire, a woman and her daughter collect potting compost from molehills on the village green. A man in Coventry finishes his thesis on bats. Eggs are delivered to the neighbours, campers moved on from Flynn's Pass. In Honolulu, an elderly lady completes the first draft of her book about her murdered friend while her husband teaches online. A woman plucks a stray hair from her nose. Mules stand in a field. A man in Bray posts a picture of an object he has thrown up into the sky. A boy falls off his bike and breaks his leg. Lilac grows. Two small children sleep in a teepee in the living room. Their mother is one of the first people in Naples to get a haircut. In California, a man films his husband playing the piano. A family's new puppy shits on the kitchen floor again. A woman in Glasgow is told not to set foot outside her door for twelve weeks. Food parcels are delivered. Teenagers make love in the back seat of a car. On the island, a woman walks through the woods in her wellingtons and a kimono. A farmer tears out two hundred metres of nesting hedgerow. Ponds are built, an origami eagle. A vet straightens a surfer's broken nose on Pendine Beach. A boy finds a crayfish in the lake. His younger sister falls headfirst out of the boat. Someone's ex dies. A girl poses in her parent's back yard. A young woman listens to birdsong outside her Leyton window. A mother of two small children is told her tumour is enflamed. Her husband cycles three times around the lake. In upstate New York, her sister pins a rhinoceros beetle in a display case. Twin girls run naked through a large house. An artist couple kiss in front of his paintings in their studio in Szczecin. Funeral services are broadcast live. In downtown Toronto, an aunt sits in her apartment surrounded by her life's work, including the coffee table. A hare runs the circuit of a yellow field. A radiologist cancels outpatients. A man cooks a lone steak on a barbeque. Someone pays ten euro for a tape of other voices to harmonise with. A sculptor chips away at a stone horse. A teacher praises her student's meticulousness. Children look blankly at their grandparents' faces.

REBECCA O'CONNOR ❧

Triptych

My daughter explains how it happened: *Grandma is your mother.*
The same sapphire eyes, set in the frames of our ages, from a line
of Irish genes: a series of sketches, as if the edges
of each of us are uncertain, our bodies
a triptych, attempts at the same idea. When
the idea of my daughter began sculpting my self-

image, I was as shocked as if I had been born with *self*
tattooed on my belly and now saw the letters ballooning: mother
in the making, wary of the crossing - less a borderline
than a no-man's land between selfhood and the mythic edge
of the world, over which women named *mothers* have fallen. Their bodies
tried to explain, in foreign tongues thick with milk, how it would be when

I split like a fruit and shivered at my baby's cry, or when,
a revenant, I would begin to remember myself.
When she opened her tiny sapphire eyes, I wanted my mother
to be the first to see her. I shone like a jewel, fulcrum in a line
of matriarchs, unaware that I'd been edged
out of the present. My mother held her, their bodies

slotting together, genes in a double helix, as the bodies
of my mother and myself did once, and I visioned her when
she sat in that hospital bed, her self
slipping away; as if from being a mother
we thought there was hope of return. Any line
separating us, any edge

between us burnt away, and freed from edges,
bearing every woman and their bodies,
I plunged into the selfless dream. Today, I am found out when
my small daughter rages: *I will do it myself!*

I can't stop my practised hands, the hands of a mother,
from fastening shoes or brushing hair; she pushes them away, a line

drawn between us, firm as those furrowed lines
of determination on her forehead, primal as the edge
of consciousness. And I see she has to love and hate me, our bodies
driven to fight suffocation. I turn bitter when
she says from her car seat *I don't need you any more, Mum*—can't stop myself
trying to sully her clarity: sharp-tongued, I say *I still need my mother*

and I'm grown up. Everyone needs their mother. I weave through the line
of traffic, recall screaming at my mum, pushing her to the edge. Our bodies
speak truth: what I say to my daughter, I say to my mother, myself.

ESTHER OTTAWAY ❧

Dye

In a menstrual cycle of balsamines
doubt revisits me.
The way it congealed
into the deer's face, eyes punctured
open by saber-toothed dread.
The balsam petal
paste on my fingernails
ages red as ruptured mouths.
There goes the green tail of August.
There goes, pollinated air.
There goes the scythe
of my mind straight into
cornstalks the height of the past.
My kitchen floor remembered the deer
shoulder you'd brought home
for three deaths in the family.
The meat, heft of gore and fur,
which my hands now seem
to have tusked through.
There goes the sun
unable to contain itself.
What kind of fear gave eyes
to the bat, only to blind.
What gave the spider four pairs.
The cornstalks billow in the rhythm
of knowing, not-knowing, between.
There goes my scythe, blade first.

SUPHIL LEE PARK

Where the Gnarled Claw Grew

(to gather: to understand; to harvest for food;
to pick up from the ground)

A gnarled claw grew out of their dislocation in the shape
of a pear tree there behind a rusty chain-link fence and

discovered the children when all the branches were
beginning again with ravenous sirens of blossoms.

They wrapped each other's fingers around the metal
chains, pressed their eyes to the gap between

to watch the tree in her strut, right there, on the other side.
They had nothing else to do. God, the sisters

on the day they chased them from the strawberry fields,
how their hunger had overwhelmed their desire

to be good and to follow the rules. That pear tree belonged
to no one, produced fruit for no farmer. They couldn't bring

themselves to clamber over the fence so early, not while
the pears were hard and tight. They gaped: pears turn out

like this? They ripened in a cleft of weeks the sun couldn't crack.
They didn't know anything. The bees came

thick when the pears fell and their tender skins broke open.
The smell, a sweet that oozed in their fingers, left them

clumsy. They could hardly bear the anxiety of want. They knew
they could get into a world of trouble. Their hunger

cussed them out and led them on until the hot day
the fence couldn't hold them back anymore and the

sharp children with their twig limbs scratched over
the barb wire, alert for the threat of an adult.

Oh, those pears: curving in toward their dark seeds
then filling out into fat hips; shades of green composed

as jars on a willing windowsill; faint brown speckles that
let slip the promise confined, the taste inside; juice that might

trickle. The bees shadowed them, lurching among
the pears and reeking of spiced liqueur and fermented sugar.

The sisters' tongues spoke quick and greedy against
the forbidden pulp. They had witnessed how the swollen

fruit could learn to detach from tree and branch—how to
offer all that flesh and juice to one flight, no matter what

the fall and the struggle of grass might bring—how to cast off
the rot of confession and to worship the sultry spoil of summer.

MICHELLE PORTER

Finding What He Can of His Own Way Home

Grand Canyon, Arizona

In memoriam, Patrick Lane (1939–2019)

There is a precision in nature.
The way air is a living thing. Taking form,
changing form. Like the spirit when it has left the body.
As though the walls of this canyon were cut
with the sharpest of tools. Wind. Sand.
Olga, my mule, prefers to walk on the brick edge
that holds the trail in place.
Beyond the edge, the canyon.
At its deepest point, the river. The body
must go with the mule. The mind must trust.
The day gathers to itself pigment, and gradations
of earth. Beyond what we imagine.
The way the heart turns inward
over the intricacies of love, and the one who has died.
We say, *Bless this man who died.*
We have carried him this far.
When the mules need to rest, we stop,
turn their heads out over the edge, into sky
as a mountain climber will swing from a solitary rope
in sleep. Bless this man as a raven
spreads its wings, an island in the air.
This one who died. As the spirit lifts and rises.
There is a sacredness, a gravity,
where the hour between present and past
is a point in the palm of the hand of air.
There is a bridge we cross, strung over the river.

Bless him. Who died, this man.
We have crossed the river with him
and do not know how to go back.

Finding what he can of his own way home—Patrick Lane, "Apples in the Rain"
Bless this man who died—Patrick Lane, "Fathers and Sons"

PAMELA PORTER ❧

Ode to McCain's Deep 'n Delicious Vanilla Cake

At 26 ingredients, it's engineered as intricately
as a vehicle, with twice the alchemic intrigue.

From the ashes of yer youth, it rises up
plastic-domed, perfectly preserved, on sale

2 for 1. In saccharine worship, your mouth
still waters, that synthetic vanilla potent,

the way imitation of a thing in nature inevitably
becomes overdone, but the garnish—delicate

chocolate tendrils—epitomizes refinery. A marvel
of 20th century technology, the frozen cake defies

time. Stretching the life of foods like the Sorcerer's Stone
for wizards would, freezers first entered Calvert kitchens

in 1950- something. If we began then to live less in
the moment, at least fewer of my cousins went to bed

hungry. The O'Tooles on The Point bought one of the earliest
fridges off analog Kijiji—just Steve Maddox, driving up

the shore, reselling goods from Fort Pepperrell out the back
of his trunk. Anyone who claims Canadian cuisine is non-existent

hasn't heard of McCain, born & raised in New Brunswick, the world's
largest retailer of frozen potatoes. Spuds for the Powers are like

a good Burgundy for the French: no meal was complete without
them, and dessert was best served from the freezer. On birthdays,

a Deep 'n Delicious was discharged from frigid storage, and leftover
candles shoved into it. You watched as yer childhood receded

like a coastline as the candles annually gave off more heat. We shifted
our faith in the 90's to scientists from bakers, because we loved

the uniformity of stiff, factory-piped icing, because his mother's
been gone so long my Dad almost forgets how her homemade bread

smeared with fresh cream & molasses tasted. Wouldn't Mary-Essie
have loved something ready-made, something she could buy

to trade for time? Unlike fallible French pastry, which ages every
sixty seconds and by day two isn't fit to bite into, one of these

bad boys maintains its integrity into infinity (or, for around six
months, which is as much of the future as is safe to bet on.)

Visit your local grocery store! This frozen cake, at its rim,
waits under fluorescents for you to carry it home. *Do not*

heat or bake. Just thaw, cut and serve. Nothing gold can
stay? Robert Frost never tried a Deep 'n Delicious cake.

MELANIE POWER ❧

Things That Are Distant but Close

A sawmill. A seiner. War's
rations and barbed wire. A garden's
trellised green beans, plots of shiso.
We plotted the temerities between.
Summer's dust blooming through
a sawmill's rotary teeth. The jar of gold

lozenges you held out to me. Later,
a book full of paper cranes. Dusk,
summer: a field burnt to curb the fires.
Goldfinches sparking between the alders.
Somewhere, smoke still curls
through your fingers. Sometimes,

a shower radio hanging from your neck,
you recited names I couldn't hear,
stooped to tend the green. Green beans.
Zucchini. The sun, a gold lighter
hung between two fingers. Shiso
embering my tongue. The smoke,

the dusty avenues, the egrets,
the ditches where the bullfrogs
swelled and murmured. Your paper
crane listing in a bowl of water
like a man-of-war aflame. The slurs
they called you then. The names

of those who left, those buried
in the interior, on a strawberry farm
across a coastal plane. No egress
for the temerities between. Your rations.
Your names. The one you stole
from a baseball player, won

from the sawmill's slick
and spinning pain. A finger. Two lungs
swollen with particulate matter.
It's fine, I never breathed it in. This,
in a tongue you only spoke indoors.
Outside, the field burns itself clean.

MICHAEL PRIOR ❧

Bird Feeder

I wait for you
Shoulder line tense and hard
Broad beaches teeter sand
I stand; a bird feeder for the stray
A pit a stop a full on monsoon
Tracing rims with fingers of doom
Once upon a time a story teller
Blowing glass into beautiful shapes
I wait for you razor clean
A hairless baby in its crate

TOMA M. RAY ❧

Massgirl

Is it cool to dedicate a book to "u know who u ahh"
Do you think the Atlantic Ocean will know I mean it
I am totally massgirl
I can't help it
I ride with the top down
I listen to Robyn
I will cut a bitch
I want to be slapped around
Pulled over
Issued a warning
Pulled over again
Spoken to sternly
I am wild to be called "YOUNG LADY"
I want to tumble from the fog of le Wednesday de Thanksgiving
The savagest night in the savagest city
I want to trickle blood from blunt force
I want my wedding ring to open my lover's jaw like a book
I want his tongue to read my braille apocalypse
I want Canadians to cower
I want other girls to wobble and puke
I run until my lungs explode
and everyone who rows the Charles can taste the blood
innard molasses copper dust
I read until the library is empty
break my face on the Timaeus
the liquid gildings, the colliding bodies
I want to be a liquid gilding, to edge us all in gold
and burn with hot metal wrath the margins of everything
I smash a bottle of wine on the toilet rim because I have no wine key
drink from the shards
Sit on the bathroom floor
Wait for security to find me

ANJULI FATIMA RAZA KOLB ❧

Timore

There is much to do when Terror strikes,
and peace to be found while the bombs ignite.
Time stops, and all your wet and welled eyes can see
are comets—frozen in space—on their tails, a dawning reality
and the impossibility of making a wish.
There is much to do when there is much to rather not.
Like poking holes on fabric as gray as your breathing is.
As still as your existence. As perforated as your vision.
Like letting fireflies glow in your abyss,
flying and glowing, glowing away.
Like making paint from agony and watching it trickle,
forming markings like the symbols of initiation upon your chest,
a painful, yet glorified rebirth.
Like taking in the pounding of the earth
and giving birth to it as your African *nana's* drums.
There are bright places, she used to say, all the bright places.
And her voice that called the war cry sings for you to not die...

There is much to do when Terror strikes,
and more to do when there is much to rather not.
Big droppings from the enemy's cattle suffocate you and
the tip-tapping of your fleeing feet threatens to break into dance.
It's true that the fires ceased to be places you were fondled.
Now they hold memories like Thich, burnt like the first dish
you made when you walked into our *boma.*
Now the fire has a smell, and your senses, long numbed
like a mutilated Southern flesh seem to work just well.
There's magic in the fire. The same fire that made you scream
let my people go gave you a voice. It scalded you
but look, heralded and tall you stand.
The voice that we demand.
There is much to feel when Terror strikes,

and senses to be awoken.
Rusty, red, rowdy blood from the blades of the foe's swords
we use to paint our sunsets.
And scared voices sing.

SAUDA SALIM ❧

alive in the second world

the blackest of wool
weaves velvety smooth
in the darkness before twilight
that rounds the four corners
absolute as nothing

this many long walks from home
I am reminded word for word
how a crowd can garble closeness
and of a need to recompose the pines
step for step like a misty form
following the bounces of my turquoise torch

the fabric of the day whorls embryonic
still nursing jet black clouds
so the constancy of my little dome
proved in an astronomical glow
by shards of shell like streaks of milk spilt

this butte having weathered
storm cloud suffusion of ominous mood
or the blurring of edges by a winter's gloom
stands as I in the skirt of its scree
losing its breath in the fall

the crystal of a civil dawn sparks
a clarifying wildfire across the sky
that the yip-howls of coyotes explain
pulls taut the warp of background
for those who muddle through frayed

and seeing me formed in that first world
and lost in the planning of passings
the red-shirted ants swirl in succession
searching for the secrets of strife

I pinch a sliver of coconut
into singular jaws

I follow behind
in a march toward my hill
with the waving of little white flags
and climb up from the darkness
and into a world of blue

I walk toward the squawking of jays

LINDSAY SEARS ❧

One Way or Another

One way or another

it will happen
because we are alive.
We animals.
We fish. We birds.
We plants.
                    Or,
it will happen
whether or not.

Stone. Mountain. Star.

MARIAN KAPLUN SHAPIRO ❧

Tomato Plant Survival Song

In a terracotta pot, ambition staked to a broken cane, and nameless
(for the lolly stick has blown away), I pull at hope without a tap root.

My character is lack: lack of vigour, lack of flower, lack
of what it is to be tomato.   The Moneymakers and Gardener's Delight
continue ravishing, predictably,

but I'll have no self-pity, no suspicions of this third-rate   third-use
potting compost.   Light and leggy as I am   yellow at the lower leaves

I'll not lament disease: I need my sugar fuels to live.

From veiny hour to hour   I live.

~

Nothing escapes me,
        woodlice roll their silver stomaches,
bees sip the sweet pea's intimate interior. The fearful caterpillar
undulates and crawls: it shall become, unless that blackbird has it.

At night when foxes screech inside their filthy quilts
I breath their musk   shit-perfume
fragrance these splotched leaves.   Season my dream.

~

Slugs!   Their terrible soft mouths.
New shoots in tatters, done for.   Why doesn't she bring salt?
Why only frowns and secateurs?

Aphids! Aphids! Look!   Their icky feet. Their hairs upon my hairs.
She lifts my blighted leaves, notices four flowers
dangling abortively and pinches them away.   No to-ma-to.

I remember that nasturtium, how it bolted, shrank, how she finally

up-ended it, broke its feeble systems in her hand.

I am alone and thirsty.

~

It persists. (On occasion now it speaks about itself in third person,
which allows for rest, and oh it wants to rest.)

There is no rest.   Grow, it whispers to its planted brain.

~

Sweet rain!   In wet light: blackbird song.

~

All day, all night, petals whisper *We'll become.*

Seed-sized bulb of green,   small machine of longing,

first dream of fruit,   hung like modest earrings

swelling then   becoming pale orange   pale red   ripe scarlet,
gladness edible.   Sing your songs for I am entering myself.
I have become tomato.

Oh tomato   I am the thing I am!

KATHRYN SIMMONDS ~

Darkness Passional

Is each turn in the ground
a mystery? What I grow reaffirms
an old trick, humus plus longing,
a formula for living in isolation

without resistance. Without forgiveness,
or praying for the body to open
at any other than its own speed.
Who else will winter in the eye of a crow?

This bedding of rods and black stems,
and absolution like a body of water
I do not know the name of, or the name
I wore when I sank to the bottom, the arcs

of my fingers a chalk smear darkening
in pulses. Who else enters when I'm
on my way to the other body, a vision
of rice field and black water and some

cloud-curious lightning like a fish's
silver belly. Transmigratory. I don't mean legumes,
or the way Pythagoras imagined the soul
folded upon itself like a library

in the umbilical protein of a bean's
wrinkly bit. I already know we are edible
and whisper to each other while eating
the ones we did not name. I mean

this repeating field where the role play
of prey and hunter ad nauseums. How many times
was I the deer, my recurring volta
through undergrowth and mulch

continuing even now on someone's screen.
If memory is just rented from the humus, then
when it's my turn in the ground
go bury me in an acre of wind.

BRIAN SNEEDEN ❧

After Walden

I am leaving out the I as if it were bread
on the grocery list, as if it were an empty egg carton
filled with soil, leaving out the I, that small soldier
of egoism. Let it out like those little painted
ladies the children grew from caterpillars,
right before a rainstorm, how they hop on the grass
and there is the dog. Isn't it beautiful:
nature wants to take, to break open
each moment, face or mouth, needle
jabbed into a bicep. Mother. How much
should we do before it's time to give a body
over to science or to ashes, to dress it in its best
things. How can the speaker ask about best
practices. We are leaving out the I,
have left the I like the child we never wanted,
in the kitchen at her grandmother's, mouth
full of dry toast asking why. We don't know why,
have never known why a man or anyone else goes
into the woods alone, what he expects to be there
when he comes back, something hot like a body or meal.
Something like a why and when. Something
to calm him. And Thoreau tells us "every man
is tasked to make his life worthy."
And it's only the women who want to go out
and claim the I like a city, which is our city,
who want to stand in the rain undone by it.

SARA MOORE WAGNER ❧

We Are One

My sister turns in the moonlight
And brushes her hand through rainbow droplets
From the falls thundering past her face.
Her hair whips wet in strands that slew over her eyes,
And snails that wait in the dark come out to slide
And twist in mossy holes amongst the rocks,
Damp with cold bells of crystal water.

My mother turns in the moonlight
Her soft silver feet treading silently,
Barely touching the fractured Earth.
Rich summer lust turns to winter memories
Cold despair creeps beneath the cool milky river,
Flooding her dreams with silence.
Standing alone she can hear
A thousand sweet voices flutter and cry
Carrying their slow bird sound far and high.

My daughter turns in the moonlight
And walks until dawn to the place
Where shells flower on the shore
And the grass on the dunes whip and bend to the squall.
Cold season gannets ragged fly,
Dip steep, fold, and plunge like arrows
Released from an empty sky.

HILARY WALKER

Lament for a Daughter

In darkness, cauled in purple wool you nest, my pale
Persephone; delicate, ephemeral spring iris
at your feet and head.

Here lies a little girl, my child, robed in gold and violet.
Asclepius, great sage of health, why could you not
forestall this grief?

The autumn fever stole her breath – season of Dionysos:
she heard the flutes and drums, and begged to dance,
but lay delirious.

We dressed her for a different feast, fresh pomegranates
at her breast, and harvest fruits for sustenance,
to sweeten parting's bitterness.

Her ivory doll we laid to rest, with sandals from the high priestess
to speed her through the asphodels, and fragrances
the priests had blessed.

May the sarcophagus guard well the gift it holds
in chill embrace, and may her spirit journey
among kindly shades, to Hesperus.

But I am desolate, bereft, estranged from life, at odds
with death: I long to share my daughter's sleep
beneath the irises.

Hellenistic sarcophagus
(from the period 323 BCE–31 BCE)
Volos Archaeological Museum, Greece

JENA WOODHOUSE ❧

CONTRIBUTORS

Amber Adams is a poet and counselor living in Boulder, Colorado. She received her MA in Literary Studies from the University of Denver, and her MA in Counseling from Regis University. Her work has appeared in *Birmingham Poetry Review*, *Narrative*, *War Literature and the Arts Journal*, *Stone Canoe Journal*, and elsewhere. She served in the United States Army Reserves and completed one tour of duty under Operation Iraqi Freedom.

Raised in Davao, **Naro Alonzo** is studying to become a clinical psychologist at the University of the Philippines – Diliman. Their poems have been published or are forthcoming in *Busilak: New LGBTQ Poetry from the Philippines* and *Tingle Anthology of Pinay Lesbian Writing*. They are also a proud talahiban-fellow of the 1st National *LGBTQ*+ Writers Workshop (https://www.pinoylgbtq.com/).

Davide Angelo's poetry has appeared in literary journals in Australia and elsewhere. He teaches English, and lives in Bendigo, Victoria, with his two daughters.

Ra Avis is an award-winning blogger, and the author of *Sack Nasty: Prison Poetry* (2016), *Dinosaur-Hearted* (2018), and *Flowers and Stars* (2018). She is a once-upon-a-time inmate, a reluctantly optimistic widow, and a generational storyteller. Ra writes regularly at Rarasaur.com.

Stuart Barnes is the author of *Glasshouses* (UQP, 2016), which won the Arts Queensland Thomas Shapcott Poetry Prize, was commended for the FAW Anne Elder Award and shortlisted for the ASAL Dame Mary Gilmore Award. He has a Bachelor of Arts in Literature and Philosophy from Monash University. From 2013–2017 he was poetry editor of *Tincture Journal*, and from 2017–2019 a program advisor for Queensland Poetry Festival. Tasmanian-born, Stuart lives in Queensland, Australia.

Jeff Bien is an internationally acclaimed poet, musician, and highly regarded meditation and consciousness teacher. His work has been published, translated, and performed in more than sixty countries. He is the author of numerous books and his poetry has been the recipient of many awards. His latest collection, *In a Time of No Song*, with an introduction by A.F. Moritz, was released by Exile Editions. Bien's inaugural CD received fraternal greetings from Leonard Cohen and accolades from other major international artists.

Mirande Bissell is a teacher in Baltimore, Maryland, and a recent graduate of Bennington College's MFA. Her first collection of poems will be published in 2021.

Michelle Bitting's fourth collection, *Broken Kingdom* won the Catamaran Prize and was named to *Kirkus Reviews*' Best of 2018. Poems appear in *The American Poetry Review, Narrative, Love's Executive Order, Tupelo Quarterly*, and others. A finalist in the 2019 *Sonora Review* and *New Millennium* Flash Prose contests, she won the 2018 Fischer Prize and Robert J. DeMott Awards. Michelle is a Lecturer in Creative Writing at Loyola Marymount University and Film Studies at Ashford U.

Yvonne Blomer is an award-winning poet and author of the critically acclaimed travel memoir, *Sugar Ride: Cycling from Hanoi to Kuala Lumpur*. Her recent poetry books are *As if a Raven* and the anthologies *Refugium: Poems for the Pacific* and *Sweet Water: Poems for the Watersheds*, Caitlin Press. Yvonne served as Victoria's poet laureate from 2015 to 2018. She lives on the traditional territories of the WSÁNEĆ peoples. www.yvonneblomer.com

Danielle Boodoo-Fortuné is a poet and visual artist from Trinidad and Tobago. Her work has been featured in publications such as *Poetry London, The Rialto, POETRY*, and the *Asian American Literary Review*. Danielle's first collection of poems, *Doe Songs*, was published by Peepal Tree Press in 2018. She was awarded the Hollick-Arvon Caribbean Writers' Prize in 2015, the Wasafiri New Writing Prize in 2016 and the OCM Bocas Prize for Poetry in 2019.

Laura Bourbonnais is a French-Canadian (Montreal native!) third-year YorkU Screenwriting and Creative Writing double major. She is the Winters Free Press Editor-in-Chief, the AMPD Journal Lead Editor, a York Her Chapter Co-Head Editor, a HOLR writing intern, and a Brick work-study student. She is a versatile artist with experience in competitive dance, music, film, theatre, and the visual arts. She strives to keep educating herself on systemic issues within and outside of Canada.

Rico Craig is a teacher, writer, and award-winning poet whose work melds the narrative, lyrical and cinematic. Craig is published widely; his poetry collection *BONE INK* (University of Western Australia Publishing) was winner of the 2017 Anne Elder Award and shortlisted for the Kenneth Slessor Poetry Prize 2018. His next collection, *Our Tongues Are Songs*, will be published in 2021. https://ricocraig.com/

Jane Craven was born and raised in North Carolina. Her poems have appeared in *The Beloit Journal*, *The Columbia Review*, *Tar River Poetry*, *The Southern Humanities Review*, and *The Carolina Quarterly*, among others. She won the Cloudbank Poetry Prize and The MacGuffin Poetry Hunt. Jane earned an MFA in Creative Writing from North Carolina State University. Her collection, *My Bright Last Country* (2020), won the Vern Rutsala Poetry Prize.

David Cruz (San José, Costa Rica 1982) was chosen as one of the most relevant poets under 40 in Spanish and included in the anthology *El canon abierto* (Visor). He has published three poetry collections. His last, *She likes to cry while listening to The Beatles*, was recently published in a bilingual edition. His poetry has also been collected in several anthologies in Latin America and Spain. His poems have been translated to Japanese, French, Portuguese, Italian. He is editor of the Rio Grande Riview at the University of Texas at El Paso.

Sadiqa de Meijer is a writer of poetry, essays, and short fiction. She was born in Amsterdam and emigrated to Canada as a child. Her poetry collections are *Leaving Howe Island* and *The Outer Wards*. Her essay collection, *alfabet/alphabet*, examines the imprint of her first language on her life in English. She also writes on themes of migration, belonging, domesticity, and landscape.

Nehassaiu deGannes, born in Trinidad & Tobago, raised in Canada and now based in New York, is an actor and poet with two chap-books, *Undressing The River*, winner of the Center For Book Arts National Letterpress Prize, *Percussion, Salt & Honey*, recipient of the Philbrick Poetry Prize, and a book-length collection, *Music For Exile*, published by Tupelo Press in 2021. Her poems have appeared in *Callaloo, Caribbean Writer, American Poetry Review* and elsewhere.

Umit Singh Dhuga is an Anglo-Indian writer and philologist based in Toronto. His poetry has appeared in *The Common, The Literary Review of Canada, Parnassus, PN Review, Rattle*, and elsewhere. He is the author of *The Sight of a Goose Going Barefoot* (2017), from which "Philoctetes at the Gym" was Highly Commended by the Forward Prizes for Poetry 2018. Dhuga holds a PhD in Classics from Columbia University.

Diane Fahey is the author of thirteen poetry collections. She has won major poetry awards and been shortlisted for seven book awards, with *Sea Wall and River Light* winning the Judith Wright Prize. She has received literary grants from the Australia Council, and the Victorian and South Australian governments. Her poetry has appeared in many international literary journals, and in over seventy anthologies. Diane holds a PhD in Creative Writing from UWS. dianefaheypoet.com

Sonia Farmer is a Bahamian writer, book artist, and publisher. Winner of the 2011 Small Axe Literary Competition, she has published several poetry collections, chapbooks, and artist's books, including *Infidelities* (longlist, 2018 OCM Bocas Prize for Caribbean Literature) and *A True & Exact History* (winner, 2019 Holle Award for Excellence in Book Arts). The founder of Poinciana Paper Press, she works with writers and artists to advance cultural ownership and voice in Caribbean narratives.

Mark Fiddes's titles *The Rainbow Factory* and *The Chelsea Flower Show Massacre* are published by Templar Poetry. Recently, he won the Oxford Brookes University International Prize, the Ruskin Prize and was placed third in the UK National Poetry Competition. His work has also appeared in *Poetry Review, POEM, The New European, The Irish Times, Magma, Aesthetica*, and *London Magazine*. He lives in temporary Brexile in the Middle East.

April Freely's work has appeared in *American Poetry Review, Ninth Letter, Gulf Coast* and elsewhere. She has received fellowships and awards from Cave Canem, the Ohio Arts Council, Vermont Studio Center, Tulsa

Artist Fellowship and Provincetown Fine Arts Work Center. She lives and works in New York City.

Catherine Graham is the author of the award-winning novel *Quarry* and six acclaimed poetry collections including *The Celery Forest*, a CBC Best Book of the Year. She teaches creative writing at University of Toronto where she won an Excellence in Teaching Award. Published internationally, she is a previous winner of TIFA's Poetry *NOW* and leads their monthly Book Club. *Æther: an out-of-body lyric* and her second novel, *The Most Cunning Heart*, are forthcoming. www.catherinegraham.com @catgrahampoet

Luke Hankins is the author of two poetry collections, *Radiant Obstacles* and *Weak Devotions*, as well as a collection of essays, *The Work of Creation*. A volume of his translations from the French of Stella Vinitchi Radulescu, *A Cry in the Snow & Other Poems*, was released by Seagull Books in 2019. He is the founder and editor of Orison Books, a non-profit literary press.

This was **Caitlin Heiligmann**'s first foray into the world of poetry! Born and raised in Montreal and currently completing an undergraduate degree in Anthropology and Political Science at McGill University, she recently rediscovered her love for creative writing and has no intention of turning back. Nearly giving into the impostor syndrome, she almost did not submit this poem—but she is very glad she did.

AE Hines is a poet who grew up in North Carolina and currently resides in Portland, Oregon. A recent Pushcart nominee, he has published widely in anthologies and literary journals such as *Potomac Review*, *Atlanta Review*, and *Hawaii Pacific Review*. He is currently at work on his first full length manuscript. www.aehines.net

Maithreyi Karnoor is the author of the novel *Sylvia: Distant Avuncular Ends*. This is the second time in a row that she is shortlisted for this prize. She was also shortlisted for the Lucien Stryk Asian Translation Prize, and has won the Kuvempu Bhasha Bharati prize for translation. She lives in India.

Victoria Korth lives in Rochester NY where she has a psychiatric practice caring for the chronically mentally ill. Poems have appeared in *Broad River Review, Ocean State Review, LEON Literary Review, Tar River Poetry,* and *Barrow Street.* The author of *Cord Color* (Finishing Line Press) and *Tacking Stitch* (forthcoming, FLP), she is working to publish her first full length manuscript. She holds an MFA from the Warren Wilson Program for Writers.

Michael Lavers is the author of *After Earth,* published by the University of Tampa Press. His poems have appeared in *Crazyhorse, 32 Poems, The Hudson Review, Best New Poets 2015, TriQuarterly, The Georgia Review,* and elsewhere. He teaches poetry at Brigham Young University.

Gregory Leadbetter is a poet and critic. He is the author of two poetry collections, *Maskwork* (2020) and *The Fetch* (2016), both with Nine Arches Press, as well as the pamphlet *The Body in the Well* (HappenStance Press, 2007), and (with photographs by Phil Thomson) *Balanuve* (Broken Sleep, 2021). He has written both poetry and radio drama for the BBC, and in 2019 five poems from *The Fetch* were set to music for piano and voice by the American composer and pianist Eric McElroy. His book *Coleridge and the Daemonic Imagination* (Palgrave Macmillan, 2011) won the University English Book Prize 2012, and he publishes widely on Romantic poetry and thought, twentieth-century and contemporary poetry. He is Professor of Poetry at Birmingham City University.

Brooke McKinney is a poet and writer from South Georgia. She is the recipient of two Academy of American Poets Awards and holds an MFA in Creative Writing from Hollins University. Her work has appeared in numerous literary journals journals such as *The Florida Review, New South, Salt Hill Journal, Potomac Review, The Southeast Review,* and *Columbia Poetry Review.* She is currently working on a memoir. Recently, she received a scholarship to the Sewanee Writers' Conference for her memoir about a thirteen-year journey with her bulldog Max. She lives with two dogs, Jane and Arlo, and a cat named Blue.

Thomas Joseph Mealey is a poet, songwriter, and artist, from Liverpool, England. He began writing his first book of poems in 2020. He is influenced by the temporary human experience and inspired by the effect it has upon memory and the changing perceptions of existence. www.thomasjosephmealey.com

Bruce Meyer is author of sixty-four books of poetry, short stories, flash fiction, and non-fiction and has eight more books forthcoming in the next three years. His most recent collection of poetry is *McLuhan's Canary* (Guernica Editions, 2019). He lives in Barrie, Ontario, and teaches at Georgian College.

Max Mitchell is currently doing a PhD in philosophy at the University of Nottingham. His research is focused on the ethical implications of things like artificial intelligence, gene editing, virtual reality, etc. Favourite novel: *Lolita*. Favourite epic poem: *The Iliad*. Favourite poem: "Ode to a Nightingale." Favourite play: *Oedipus Rex*. Favourite pastoral romance: *My Ántonia*. Favourite old, boring classic: *Madame Bovary*. In his free time he likes to lift weights and spy on people through his binoculars.

Shane Neilson is a disabled poet, physician, and critic who lives in Oakville. His *Dysphoria* (PQL, 2017) was awarded the Hamilton Literary Award for Poetry in 2018 and *New Brunswick* won a best book award from *The Miramichi Reader* in 2020. He is the festival director of the AbleHamilton Poetry Festival. His poems have appeared in *Poetry Magazine*, the *Walrus*, and *Verse Daily*.

Dianty Ningrum is an Indonesian currently residing in Naarm (Melbourne) completing her doctoral degree in sustainable development. She has been published in *The Scores Journal* and *Australia Poetry Anthology*.

Damen O'Brien is an Australian poet writing in Brisbane, Queensland. Damen has won or been shortlisted in many poetry competitions in Australia and internationally including the Peter Porter Poetry Prize and the Moth Poetry Prize. His poems have appeared in *Cordite*, *StylusLit*, *Southerly*, *Island*, and many others. Damen's first poetry book will be published in 2021. www.dameno.org

Rebecca O'Connor's debut collection *We'll Sing Blackbird* was shortlisted for the Irish Times Shine Strong Award. She is the recipient of a Geoffrey Dearmer Prize and was a poet-in-residence at the Wordsworth Trust. Her debut novel, *He Is Mine and I Have No Other*, was published by Canongate in 2018 and shortlisted for the Kate O'Brien Award. She lives in rural Ireland with her husband and three children, and is co-director of The Moth (www.themothmagazine.com).

Esther Ottaway is an award-winning Australian poet who often writes about women's experiences. Her poetry features in the noted anthology *Thirty Australian Poets* and in leading newspapers, literary journals and anthologies. Her book *Blood Universe: poems on pregnancy* was critically acclaimed. Her second collection will be released in 2021, with a third collection, *She Doesn't Seem Autistic*, also forthcoming. Her work is online at https://esther-ottaway-poet.jimdosite.com. She lives in the island state of Tasmania.

Suphil Lee Park is a bilingual writer who grew up in South Korea. She holds a BA in English from NYU and an MFA in Poetry from UT Austin. Her poetry has appeared or is forthcoming in *Colorado Review*, *Denver Quarterly*, *Ploughshares*, *the Massachusetts Review*, and *the Missouri Review*, among many others. Her fiction is forthcoming in *J Journal*, *Storm Cellar*, and *the Iowa Review*.

Michelle Porter's first book of poetry, *Inquiries*, was shortlisted for the Pat Lowther Memorial Award for Best Book of Poetry in Canada in 2019. *Approaching Fire* is her newest book—a creative nonfiction exploration of the history of her great-grandfather, who was a Métis fiddler. She is a citizen of the Métis Nation and member of the Manitoba Metis Federation. She currently lives in St. John's, Newfoundland and Labrador.

Pamela Porter's work has won more than a dozen provincial, national and international awards, including the Governor General's Award for her young adult novel *The Crazy Man*, as well as the Pat Lowther, Raymond Souster, and the CBC/Canada Writes shortlists. Among her 14 published books, her most recent is *Likely Stories*, released in 2019 from Ronsdale Press. Pamela lives near Sidney, BC with her family and a menagerie of rescued horses, dogs, and cats.

Melanie Power is a Montreal-based writer from St. John's, Newfoundland. Her poetry has been published in various Canadian literary journals. Other work has been longlisted for the CBC Poetry Prize, and shortlisted in poetry contests by *Arc Magazine*, *The Malahat Review*, and *The Antigonish Review*. She is a recent graduate of Concordia University's MA in English Literature & Creative Writing. www.melaniedpower.com

Michael Prior is a writer and teacher. His poems have appeared in *The New Republic*, *Poetry*, *Narrative*, *Poetry Northwest*, *PN Review*, The Asian American Writers' Workshop's *The Margins*, and the Academy of American Poets' *Poem-A-Day* series. His first full-length collection, *Model Disciple* (Véhicule Press, 2016), was named one of the best books of the year by the CBC. His second book, *Burning Province* (McClelland & Stewart/ Penguin Random House), was published in Spring 2020.

Born in Russia, raised in Israel, **Toma M. Ray** has called Montreal home since 2006. Childhood memories include the opera house (off stage and on) in Tel-Aviv. Writing has been a lifelong pursuit and passion. A polyglot, Toma writes in several languages. Flowing from a body of work in Hebrew, this poem is a part of Toma's debut work in English.

Anjuli Fatima Raza Kolb is a poet, translator, and scholar of postcolonial literature and theory. Her poems and essays have appeared in venues including the *Poetry Foundation*, the *Boston Review*, *FENCE*, *Critical Quarterly*, the *Los Angeles Review of Books*, and more. Her scholarly book, *Epidemic Empire* is forthcoming from the University of Chicago Press in late 2020. She teaches at the University of Toronto and lives in New York.

Sauda Salim was born and raised in Mombasa, Kenya. She is a second-year student of International Relations and a poetry enthusiast. Currently working at the University of Pennsylvania's Kelly Writers House, Sauda channels her passion for poetry by supporting poetry events in Philadelphia, and both Swahili and English poetry back home.

Lindsay Sears joins the writing community after serving as a mental health nurse in the U.S. Navy. She and her husband spend long, hot summers in Alabama with family. They explore and hike the wilderness the rest of the year.

Marian Kaplun Shapiro is the author of a professional book, *Second Childhood* (Norton, 1988), a poetry book, *Players in the Dream, Dreamers In The Play* (Plain View Press, 2007) and two chapbooks: *Your Third Wish*, (Finishing Line, 2007); and *The End of the World, Announced On Wednesday* (Pudding House, 2007). A five-time Senior Poet Laureate of Massachusetts, where she lives and practices as a psychologist, she was nominated for the

Pushcart Prize in 2012. Her latest book of experimental poems, *At the Edge of the Cliff*, was published by Plain View Press in January 2021.

Kathryn Simmonds has published two collections of poetry, 'Sunday at the Skin Launderette' (2008), and 'The Visitations' (2013). She lives with her family in Norwich, a small medieval city in the east of England.

Brian Sneeden is the author of *Last City* (Carnegie Mellon University Press, 2018). His poetry has received the *Iowa Review* Award for Poetry, the *Indiana Review* 1/2K Prize, and other awards. His translation of Phoebe Giannisi's *Homerica* (World Poetry Books, 2017) was selected by Anne Carson as a favorite book of 2017; his translation of Giannisi's collection, *Cicada*, is forthcoming from New Directions. He is Program Coordinator of Translation Studies at the University of Connecticut.

Sara Moore Wagner is the recipient of a 2019 Sustainable Arts Foundation award, and the author of the chapbooks *Tumbling After* (forthcoming from Red Bird Chapbooks, 2021) and *Hooked Through* (2017). Her poetry has appeared or is forthcoming in many journals including *Cimarron*, *Third Coast*, *Poet Lore*, *Waxwing*, *The Cincinnati Review*, and *Nimrod*, among others. She has been nominated multiple times for the Pushcart prize, and Best of the Net.

Hilary Walker: "I was ten when one of my poems appeared in the Edinburgh *Evening News*. I knew then that poetry was important to me. I do an ordinary office job, but my mind is full of words and images. In August my world shattered when fire destroyed my home after a lightning strike. A week later I received news that I had been shortlisted for the Montreal Prize. Perfect timing; I'm still smiling."

Jena Woodhouse, based in Queensland, Australia, is the author/ translator/ co-compiler of ten book and chapbook publications in various genres, five of which are poetry collections, most recently *The Book of Lost Addresses: A retrospective* (Picaro Poets 2020). Her poems were shortlisted for the Montreal International Poetry Prize in 2013 and 2015. Having lived and worked in Greece for ten years, she draws on that source as a site of continuing revelation and inspiration.

EDITORS

Jordan Abel is a Nisga'a writer from Vancouver. He is the author of *The Place of Scraps* (winner of the Dorothy Livesay Poetry Prize), *Un/inhabited*, and *Injun* (winner of the Griffin Poetry Prize). Abel's latest project *NISHGA* is a deeply personal and autobiographical book that attempts to address the complications of contemporary Indigenous existence and the often invisible intergenerational impact of residential schools. Abel recently completed a PhD at Simon Fraser University, and is currently working as an Assistant Professor in the Department of English and Film Studies at the University of Alberta.

Kaveh Akbar's poems appear in *The New Yorker*, *Poetry*, *The New York Times*, *Paris Review*, and elsewhere. He is the author of *Pilgrim Bell* (Graywolf 2021) and *Calling a Wolf a Wolf* (Alice James 2017). Kaveh was born in Tehran, Iran, and teaches at Purdue University and in the low resi-dency MFA programs at Randolph College and Warren Wilson.

CAConrad received a 2019 Creative Capital grant to complete their nationwide (Soma)tic poetry ritual titled, "Resurrect Extinct Vibration." They also received a Pew Fellowship in the Arts, as well as The Believer Magazine Book Award and The Gil Ott Book Award. Their nine books of poetry and essays include *While Standing in Line for Death* (Wave Books), which won the 2018 Lambda Book Award. They teach regularly at Columbia University in New York City, and Sandberg Art Institute in Amsterdam. For more on their books and the documentary *The Book of Conrad* from Delinquent Films, see http://caconrad.blogspot.com/.

Wendy Cope was born in Erith, Kent UK. After reading history at Oxford, she worked as a primary school teacher in London until the publication of her first book, *Making Cocoa for Kingsley Amis*, in 1986. Since then she has been freelance. Her fifth collection of poems, *Anecdotal Evidence*, was published in 2018. She has also written for children and edited several anthologies. She was awarded an OBE for services to literature in 2010.

Susan Elmslie's second poetry collection, *Museum of Kindness* (Brick, 2017), was shortlisted for the Quebec Writers' Federation A.M. Klein

Poetry Prize and the League of Canadian Poets' Pat Lowther Memorial Award. Her first collection, *I, Nadja, and Other Poems* (Brick, 2006), won the Klein Prize and was shortlisted for the McAuslan First Book Prize. Her poems have appeared in many Canadian magazines, anthologies, and in a prize-winning chapbook, *When Your Body Takes to Trembling* (Cranberry Tree, 1996). Her work has been supported by the Canada Council for the Arts and she has been a resident at the Banff Centre for the Arts and at Hawthornden Castle in Scotland.

Steven Heighton's most recent poetry collection, *The Waking Comes Late*, received the 2016 Governor General's Award. In 2019 he was a finalist for The Moth Prize, based in Ireland, for "Christmas Work Detail, Samos." His poetry and fiction have received four gold National Magazine Awards and have appeared in the *London Review of Books*, *Poetry*, *Tin House*, *Best American Poetry*, *Zoetrope*, TLR, *Agni*, *The Walrus*, *London Magazine*, *New England Review*, and several editions of *Best Canadian Poetry*. He also writes fiction, most recently the novel *The Nightingale Won't Let You Sleep*. An earlier novel, *Afterlands*, was a NYTBR editors' choice and was cited on year-end lists in the US, the UK, and Canada. Heighton is also a translator and occasional fiction reviewer for the NYTBR.

Yusef Komunyakaa's books of poetry include *Taboo, Dien Cai Dau, Thieves of Paradise, Neon Vernacular*, for which he received the Pulitzer Prize, *Pleasure Dome, Talking Dirty to the Gods, Warhorses, The Chameleon Couch, Testimony, The Emperor of Water Clocks*, and *Everyday Mojo Songs of Earth*. His honours include the William Faulkner Prize (Université Rennes, France), the Ruth Lilly Poetry Prize, and the Wallace Stevens Award. His plays, performance art, and libretti include *The Deacons, Wakonda's Dream, Saturnalia, Testimony, Gilgamesh: A Verse Play*, and *Somewhere Near Here (Bright Darkness)*. He is Distinguished Senior Poet and Global Professor at New York University.

John Leonard was born in the UK and came to Australia in 1991. He completed a PhD at the University of Queensland and was poetry editor of *Overland* (Melbourne) from 2003 to 2007. He has six collections of poetry, the most recent being *Wordfall*. His poetry has been translated into French, Croatian, Spanish and Chinese and published in those versions.

Eli MacLaren teaches poetry, Canadian literature, and the history of books and publishing in the Department of English at McGill University. He is the author of *Dominion and Agency: Copyright and the Structuring of the Canadian Book Trade, 1867–1918* (University of Toronto Press, 2011) and *Little Resilience: The Ryerson Poetry Chap-Books* (McGill-Queen's University Press, 2020).

Marilène Phipps was born and grew up in Haiti. She is a recipient of the NAACP's Award of Excellence for outstanding commitment in advancing the culture and causes for communities of colour. Phipps has held fellowships at the Guggenheim Foundation, Harvard's Bunting Institute, the W.E.B. Du Bois Institute for Afro-American Research, and the Center for the Study of World Religions. Her collection, *The Company of Heaven*, won the 2010 Iowa Short Fiction Award. Her poetry won the 1993 Grolier prize, and her collection, *Crossroads and Unholy Water*, won the 2000 Crab Orchard Poetry Prize. Her memoir, *Unseen Worlds*, was released in 2019 by Calumet Editions. Her new novel, *House of Fossils*, was released by Calumet Editions in 2020.

Sridala Swami is a poet, essayist and photographer. Her first collection of poems, *A Reluctant Survivor* (2007), was published by the Sahitya Akademi / National Academy of Letters (India). Swami has written four books for children, published by Pratham Books in 2009 and 2012. She was the 2011 Charles Wallace writer-in-residence at the University of Stirling, Scotland, and was a Fellow of the International Writing Program at the University of Iowa, 2013. Swami's second collection of poetry, *Escape Artist*, published by the Aleph Book Company (2014), is the first book to appear under the aegis of the Jehangir Sabavala Foundation (JSF).

Gillian Sze is the author of multiple poetry collections, including *Peeling Rambutan*, *Redrafting Winter*, and *Panicle*, which were finalists for the Quebec Writers' Federation A.M. Klein Prize for Poetry. She studied Creative Writing and English Literature at Concordia University and received a Ph.D. in Études anglaises from Université de Montréal. Her first picture book, *The Night is Deep and Wide*, is a bedtime poem and will be published by Orca Book in 2021. Originally from Winnipeg, she now resides in Montreal where she teaches creative writing and literature.

Véhicule Press